LAMP LIGHT
Living

"Acknowledge and take to heart this day that the Lord is God in heaven above and on the earth below. There is no other. Keep his decrees and commands, which I am giving you today, so

THAT IT MAY GO *Well*

with you and your children after you and that you may live long in the land the Lord your God gives you for all time."

Deuteronomy 4:39-40

Created with an appreciation for both the Old & New Testaments

"Children, obey your parents in the Lord, for this is right. 'Honor your father and mother"—which is the first commandment with a promise—

THAT IT MAY GO *Well*

and that you may enjoy long life on the earth.'"

Ephesians 6:1-3

 Please share and tag @lampandlightliving, thank you!

The Poached Egg

Much of what I learned from books in school has been long forgotten. Many of the things I read year after year in textbooks simply were memorized to pass a class and then forgotten. However, the things I put into practice I retained. I find this to be true even as an adult.

The Story of the Poached Egg:

I've never poached an egg. I love to cook and I've made eggs many ways, but never poached. A few months back I decided I wanted to poach an egg. So, I read all about it. I found this great article with many methods of poaching an egg, the pros and cons of different techniques, and some really useful tips.
I was ready to poach an egg!
But I never did.
Recently, I watched a show with my husband in which there was a beautifully poached egg on top of avocado toast. Suddenly I remembered: I never poached an egg! I still want to!
I remember reading an article about it, but I never followed through and did anything with that information. So the truth is I've forgotten nearly all of it. Now if ever I truly poach an egg, I will need to reread all of the information. Had I simply poached one egg, I would indeed know how to poach an egg.

This is a silly story to illustrate a point. In our culture, we are accustomed to the idea that if you read and study something you know something. However, until you really put it into practice, you don't know a whole lot. We can read about how to do a job or we can actually can do a job.
I spent 10 years as a hairstylist. I did not learn to do hair from a textbook. I learned to do hair by doing hair. I could hand you my textbook from hair school and you could read it. But that would not make you a hairstylist. True knowledge comes by doing.
Our job as parents who want to prepare our children for a Christ-like life is to take what we read in a book and apply it to our real lives with action. It is to teach beyond pages! My hope is that this curriculum will aid you in doing that.
Enjoy your time teaching your children. Ask the Lord for creative ways to do something with what you know and what you teach your children!

Faith comes by hearing. Faith without works is dead. Do something with what you know and train your children to do the same!

TABLE OF
Contents

CURRICULUM
Overview

That It May Go Well is designed to work well for homeschooling multiple children. It is a hybrid approach combining unit studies, living books, nature studies, responsible use of technology, and structured learning. It is a Bible-based approach to homeschooling. You will simply need to add a math curriculum and some favorite books to be ready to start learning. (Our family uses Math-U-See which is a 30-week program.)

Bible-based

The foundation and core of this curriculum is the Bible. It is the most important book you will use.

6 unit studies, 5 weeks each

This curriculum is broken up into 6 unit studies that are 5 weeks each. The first four weeks are structured with worksheets and all information provided. The fifth week is a personal unit study that you create with your child to study something of interest with them. A basic outline is provided for week 5.

4 days a week

Structured schooling takes place four days a week. Consider adding field trips or extra curricular activities to round out a five day week.

Science follows the days of creation

Each day of creation God created something unique. This provides the outline for Science for each unit.

Living books

A personal collection of books or library access is helpful. Living books are an important part of this curriculum and are used for historical studies and personal reading.

ADDITIONAL
Information

Spelling-
Your child's spelling words (grades 1+) are pulled from your child's writing. Edit their writing each day and add words that are spelled incorrectly to the following week's spelling list provided at the beginning of each unit. The goal is that they practice words they truly struggle with, and that spelling becomes a part of writing, not just a list to memorize and forget.

Vocabulary-
For grades 2 and up, vocabulary is incorporated into their workbooks.

HISTORY-
It is recommended that you choose historical books to read with your children. Grades 2 and up will have a writing assignment on a historical figure. If you decide not to incorporate historical reading, simply do research on a person in history or use a person from the Bible. Missionary biographies are great choices. Aim to read one every two weeks to stay on schedule with writing assignments.

Removable Charts-
Throughout this curriculum, you will find some charts that are intended for removal, if you wish. Feel free to hang them in your school area or allow your child to view them. You may wish to laminate these to preserve for future use.

Handwriting-
If your child needs additional handwriting practice beyond what is provided in their student workbook, we highly recommend the curriculum *A Reason for Handwriting*. Please be sure your children are forming letters starting at the top and following correct penmanship routines. Proper pencil positioning, paper slant, and sitting correctly all play into penmanship. Another helpful curriculum if you need a refresher on letter formation is *Handwriting Without Tears*. They have downloads available that demonstrate letter formation.

Practical Learning-
This information repeats through the units. For grades K-2 you may wish to reduce the amount of information you require them to remember. Once a fact is memorized you may skip this and review as needed.

*NOTE: Please check your students book each day, some lessons have notes to parents.

Welcome!

Let's take a moment to set our hearts on God and commit all our ways to Him. Let's give Him authority over our homeschooling journey and over our parenting.
Our job as Christian parents is to raise kids who fear the Lord and seek first His kingdom and His righteousness.

God is the Creator of the world and the One Who defines the laws of what He created. He created the sun to move in a specific order, yet He also made it stand still. He created rivers to flow downstream, yet He caused the Jordan river to heap up so there would be a dry path for His people. Time and time again, the Bible is a story of God creating order and systems but having the power to cause that order to submit to Him.

God defeats enemies, frees prisoners, and changes reality.
Those who fear God and follow Him have extraordinary wisdom and guidance from the Holy Spirit. Jesus is a firm foundation and the Light of life. As Christian parents, this truth follows us into our children's education.

We must believe God and the entirety of His Word. The book of James says that those who ask for wisdom without doubting will receive wisdom from God. However, those who doubt are like waves of the sea, blown and tossed by the wind, and they should not suppose they will receive anything from the Lord. Please take a moment to set your heart on the Lord, confess this statement, and pray this prayer.

God, I believe you. I take you at your Word and I believe that everything you say is true. I believe that wisdom comes from fearing you. I believe you can give knowledge to me and to my children. You are who you say you are. You can do all that you say you can do. You did all that Your Word says that you did.

Father,

Thank you that you have called me to lay aside the ways of the world and to follow you. Help me and my entire family to love you with all of our heart, soul, and strength. Please give me the wisdom that I need for this home school year. I bless and praise Your mighty name! Amen.

We have been ingrained with and indoctrinated by the thought that wisdom and learning come through textbooks, schools, and higher education institutions, but the Bible does not agree. If the world is where we go for wisdom and knowledge, we are essentially disagreeing with God through our actions. The most important book we need is the Bible. If we had nothing else, God could help us by the power of the Holy Spirit to teach our children. God speaks much in His Word about training our children and impressing His ways upon them.

I want to share some foundational Scriptures that formulated my mindset on deciding to make the move toward using the Bible as my primary text.

"May grace and peace be multiplied to you in the knowledge of God and of Jesus our Lord. **His divine power has granted to us all things that pertain to life and godliness, through the knowledge of him who called us to his own glory and excellence**, by which he has granted to us his precious and very great promises, so that through them you may become partakers of the divine nature, having escaped from the corruption that is in the world because of sinful desire. For this very reason, make every effort to supplement your faith with virtue, and virtue with knowledge, and knowledge with self-control, and self-control with steadfastness, and steadfastness with godliness, and godliness with brotherly affection, and brotherly affection with love. For if these qualities are yours and are increasing, they keep you from being ineffective or unfruitful in the knowledge of our Lord Jesus Christ. For whoever lacks these qualities is so nearsighted that he is blind, having forgotten that he was cleansed from his former sins. Therefore, brothers, be all the more diligent to confirm your calling and election, for if you practice these qualities you will never fall. For in this way there will be richly provided for you an entrance into the eternal kingdom of our Lord and Savior Jesus Christ."
2 Peter 1:2-11 ESV [Bold emphasis mine]

"The fear of the LORD is the beginning of wisdom, and knowledge of the Holy One is understanding."
Proverbs 9:10

If God's Word can be believed (and it can!), then God's divine power gives us all we need for life and godliness. Our job is to know Him who called us! We know Him by His Word and by seeking Him with all our heart, soul, and strength. We listen for His voice, and we obey.

Our children will face those who do not believe God exists, those who distort truth, those who worship false gods, and many other challenges in their lives. Not only do they need to remain firm in their own faith, but they also need to be a light to those around them and share the Good News of Jesus with the world. There is no one more equipped than a God-fearing mother and father to teach their children. When we doubt, we should come back to what God defines as wise. Wisdom is found in the fear of the LORD. A secular school system that has gone to great lengths to remove God is not the answer. They will not teach our children fear of the LORD. The world may say they are wise, and by their standards perhaps they are, but by our standards, anyone who does not place their trust and hope in God does not have the wisdom of God.

"For the message of the cross is foolishness to those who are perishing, but to us who are being saved it is the power of God. For it is written:
'I will destroy the wisdom of the wise;
the intelligence of the intelligent I will frustrate.'
Where is the wise person? Where is the teacher of the law? Where is the philosopher of this age? Has not God made foolish the wisdom of the world? For since in the wisdom of God the world through its wisdom did not know him, God was pleased through the foolishness of what was preached to save those who believe. Jews demand signs and Greeks look for wisdom, but we preach Christ crucified: a stumbling block to Jews and foolishness to Gentiles, but to those whom God has called, both Jews and Greeks, Christ the power of God and the wisdom of God. For the foolishness of God is wiser than human wisdom, and the weakness of God is stronger than human strength.
Brothers and sisters, think of what you were when you were called. Not many of you were wise by human standards; not many were influential; not many were of noble birth. But God chose the foolish things of the world to shame the wise; God chose the weak things of the world to shame the strong. God chose the lowly things of this world and the despised things—and the things that are not—to nullify the things that are, so that no one may boast before him. It is because of him that you are in Christ Jesus, who has become for us wisdom from God—that is, our righteousness, holiness and redemption. Therefore, as it is written: 'Let the one who boasts boast in the Lord.'"
1 Corinthians 1:18-31

Please don't set your heart on the world's "wisdom" that says Jesus is not the Savior of the world. He is. And Jesus is the way, the truth, and the life! You can use the Word of God to teach and train your children for all that they need for life and godliness. Do not be afraid! The Holy Spirit God will direct all your paths and give you what you need to equip your family.

SYMBOL
Guide

 Please listen to and worship God with this song.

 Marks a section where there is a task to complete in your student(s) workbook or otherwise.

 Recommended reading time

 Art/handicraft project. For visuals of these, check out Lamp and Light Living on Pinterest. Our goal with arts and crafts is to value our children's time and resources to create projects that are worth keeping and will not be discarded quickly. Modify these to use what you have and enjoy. Do not undervalue the internet. YouTube and Pinterest provide awesome ways to learn to do projects. If your child has other handicrafts they wish to learn or want to practice feel free to substitute those in for the art provided.

 Prayer time

 Observe science in creation.

 A video recommendation found on YouTube for free. These are optional. If you opt out of the science videos, be prepared to replace them with your own research and/or books.

*Note
I audited the science videos one by one and I do **not** recommend all videos from the channels I shared. I skipped videos that shared things that were contrary to Biblical truth, mentioned evolution, or had other non-Biblical worldviews.

CURRICULUM
Planner

LIBRARY LIST Plan to visit the library at the beginning of each unit.

- [ ] Child's Atlas that includes information about continents
- [ ] Book about the continent and country you will be studying
- [ ] 2 Historical Figure Books (optional: theme with the continent study)
- [ ] Age-appropriate books for each child's individual reading

PREP LIST

- [ ] Bible (One for each child that can read, one for yourself.)
- [ ] Map or Globe
- [ ] That It May Go Well printed grade appropriate worksheets
- [ ] Access to the Internet and YouTube
- [ ] An outdoor space for observation walks
- [ ] Stamps & envelopes for mailing letters
- [ ] Basic art supplies
- [ ] Supplies for your child(ren) for their handicraft of choice

OPTIONAL EXTRAS

- [ ] A binder for each child to store visual reports
- [ ] A notebook to turn into a recipe book
- [ ] Scrapbooking supplies/stickers for visual reports

MASTER
Supply List

I recommend that you glance at this before each unit so you will be aware of what may be needed beyond basic household items. Remember, this curriculum works for you and your family and can be modified as needed.

UNIT 1

- [ ] Rocks
- [ ] Rocks painting supplies

UNIT 2

- [ ] Key chain
- [ ] Macrame supplies
- [ ] Supplies to make a basket
- [ ] Wire & rock for photo holder

UNIT 3

- [ ] 3 fruits with seeds (week 1)
- [ ] Rope or scarlet cord for knot tying
- [ ] Soil & seeds (herbs are a good choice)
- [ ] Laminator (helpful, not necessary)
- [ ] Tin can
- [ ] Modge podge & fabric or paint
- [ ] Dried flower, ribbon
- [ ] Hole punch
- [ ] Variety of veggies (see week 3, day 3)
- [ ] Ingredients for "dirt" pudding, including gummy worms if desired

UNIT 4

- [ ] Supplies for making a Bible game
- [ ] Grapes & toothpicks
- [ ] Play-dough, teaspoon & tablespoon
- [ ] Cookie dough, cookie decorating supplies (see week 4)

UNIT 5

- [ ] Rocks & paint
- [ ] Coffee filter, coffee grounds
- [ ] Fan, paper
- [ ] Card-making supplies

UNIT 6

- [ ] Bible study supplies
- [ ] Cardboard & markers
- [ ] Sign making (see week 3)
- [ ] Measuring tape, scale, ink
- [ ] Supplies for bird feeder (see week 4)

UNIT
One

UNIT
Resources

UNIT VERSE

Say this verse when prompted with your kids. The goal with this verse is not perfect memorization in younger grades. The goal is Scripture truth being on their heart and mind.

*Aim for weekly memory verses to be quoted by each child and written from memory for grades 4-5.

"You see, at just the right time, when we were still powerless, Christ died for the ungodly. Very rarely will anyone die for a righteous person, though for a good person someone might possibly dare to die. But God demonstrates his own love for us in this: While we were still sinners, Christ died for us."
Romans 5:6-8

PRAYER REQUESTS

Record things you and your children would like to pray over here. Be sure to check back and praise the Lord when He answers. Prompt your kids to think about praying for others. Read Matthew 6:9-13 for how Jesus taught us to pray. As you study the Word, notice the pattern of Biblical prayers and prayer requests, and try to learn from the Word.

_____   _____

_____   _____

_____   _____

_____   _____

_____   _____

 ♫ All of Creation- Mercy Me

Read to student:

Welcome to our new school year! Are you excited? Can you tell me something you are excited to learn this year? What is something you hope we will study? (Allow student to respond.)

I am excited for this year! I am excited to teach you and help you learn lots of new things. What I am most excited about is seeking God and studying His Word with you. We are going to be reading the Bible and learning how to live our lives to be pleasing to God. We are going to learn many other amazing things about God's world and the people who live in God's world. We are going to hide God's Word in our hearts. Psalm 119:11 says, "I have hidden your word in my heart that I might not sin against you." Hiding God's Word in our hearts helps us to obey Him. I want you to love God so much that you want to walk with Him, listen to Him, and obey Him! Are you ready to read about God creating the earth? We are going to start reading the Bible today. You may color a picture in the space in your book while I read. Pay attention to what I read because I want you to tell me the story in your own words when I finish reading. (Show student the space for drawing a picture in their workbook.)

 Please pray with your kids. Encourage them to pray also.

Scripture Memory Genesis 1:1-2 Have your children say this with you.

"In the beginning God created the heavens and the earth.
Now the earth was formless and empty, darkness was over the surface
of the deep, and the Spirit of God was hovering over the waters."

 While you read the Bible, have your kids color their sheet in their workbook.

 Bible Reading: Genesis 1-2

Have the student(s) tell back what you read. Offer help along the way and kindly explain what you expect when they tell back a story. Be encouraging and compliment them.

 Handwriting practice

Review

- Say the ABCs
- (1st +) Do you remember what nouns and verbs are? (Noun- person, place, or thing. Verb- a word that shows action.)
- (1st +) When do we capitalize the first letter of a word? (Beginning of a sentence, proper noun, and the word I.)
- We are going to learn (practice) the calendar. Do you know how many days are in a week? How about how many months are in a year? Say the days of the week and the months of the year.

 Language Arts Section in Student Workbook

Read to student:

Today we learned that God created the heavens and the earth in six days. That is pretty amazing! One week and God created everything! What did God create on day one? Do you remember? Did you notice that God did not create the sun, moon, and stars until day 4? It is interesting that separating light from dark was the first thing that He did. How do you think that is possible? The Bible says that God is light and in Him is no darkness at all. Jesus also said that He is the light of the world and that no one who walks with Him is in darkness. We know that Jesus was with God in the beginning. It is hard to understand, but God, Jesus, and the Holy Spirit are one. They were all in the beginning at Creation. You will learn more about this later. Some things in the Bible are hard to understand, but we can trust everything it says because it is God's Word.

 Follow the Creation Scavenger Hunt in your student's workbook. Please save the items collected from creation for future projects.

 Read out loud to your children. This is a great time to read historical books. Be sure to choose books that are written from a Christian perspective or audit them closely for anything that isn't God glorifying and true. Children grades 1-5 should also spend time reading age-appropriate books.

CHECK LIST

- [ ] Worship
- [ ] Read Genesis 1-2
- [ ] Creation Scavenger Hunt
- [ ] Individual reading/reading out loud
- [ ] Complete worksheets with each child
- [ ] Math of choice

WEEK 1, DAY 2

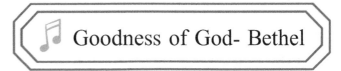

Read to student:

Do you remember what we learned yesterday? What is your favorite thing that God created? Today we are going to learn about something sad. When we disobey God that is called sin. We are going to learn about when sin entered the world. One of the ways that we can avoid sin is by memorizing and obeying God's Word. When we know what God says, we can obey God and avoid sin. We all sin and fall short of God's standard and His glory. When we sin, we have forgiveness through Jesus. Everyone sins. The only person on earth who never disobeyed God was Jesus. Have you chosen to accept Jesus and salvation through Him? That is the most important decision you will ever make. I want to make sure that you have salvation through Jesus and that you know how to tell other people about Jesus. Sharing the Gospel (that's the good news that Jesus is our Savior) is very important. God wants us to share about Jesus because He does not want anyone to die in their sins and be separated from Him for eternity. Because knowing God's Word is so important, we are going to work on memorizing it through your weekly verse and also through some longer sections of Scripture that we will say each school day together.

 Please pray with your kids. Encourage them to pray also.

Scripture Memory Romans 5:6-8 Found at the beginning of this unit.

> Scripture Memory Genesis 1:1-2 Have your children say this with you.
>
> "In the beginning God created the heavens and the earth.
> Now the earth was formless and empty, darkness was over the surface of the deep, and the Spirit of God was hovering over the waters."

 While you read the Bible have your kids color their sheet in their workbook.

Bible Reading: Genesis 3-4

Have the student(s) tell back what you read. Offer help along the way and kindly explain what you expect when they tell back a story. Be encouraging and compliment them.

 Handwriting practice

Practical Learning   Have students repeat these facts after you.

- There are 24 hours in a day, 60 minutes in an hour, and 60 seconds in a minute.
- There are 52 weeks in a year and 7 days in a week.
- "Thirty days hath September, April, June, and November; all the rest have 31 except February which has 28, except on leap year when it has 29."
- There are 365 days in a year, and a leap year has 366.

✓ Language Arts Section in Student Workbook

Read to student:

Do you know what a continent is? A continent is a continuous expanse of land. There are 7 continents on earth. Africa, Antarctica, Asia, Australia, Europe, North America, and South America. Do you know which continent you live on? (Help child with the answer.)

We are going to look at a globe (or map) and I am going to show you the continents. About 71% of the earth is covered by water! There are 5 oceans that make up the majority of that water. The Arctic Ocean, the Southern Ocean, the Indian Ocean, the Atlantic Ocean, and the Pacific Ocean. Have you ever been to the ocean? Which one? Can you describe what it is like near the ocean? (Encourage 5 senses)

We are going to learn more about continents this year, and more importantly about the people who live on each continent.

Look at a globe or map with your child. Show them each continent, ocean, and help them locate where you live.

Complete the worksheets in their student workbook.

Read out loud to your children, this is a great time to read historical books. Be sure to choose books that are written from a Christian perspective or audit them closely for anything that isn't God glorifying and true. Children grades 1-5 should also spend time reading age-appropriate books.

CHECK LIST

- ☐ Worship
- ☐ Bible Reading
- ☐ Complete worksheets with each child
- ☐ Individual reading/reading out loud
- ☐ Math of choice

WEEK 1, DAY 3

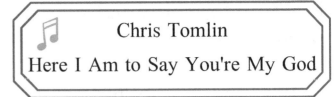
♫ Chris Tomlin
Here I Am to Say You're My God

Read to student:

Are you ready to learn some amazing things today? Remember how we learned that sin entered the world because Adam and Eve disobeyed God? God had a plan for sin. We have been reading from the Old Testament. The Bible is divided into two parts. The Old Testament (OT) and the New Testament (NT). The OT tells the story from Creation up through the prophets who foretold of Jesus' coming. The NT starts with Jesus and goes all the way through Revelation, a prophecy of what is still to come! Both the OT and the NT make up the Bible. Every part of the Bible is very important! We are going to learn how they connect beautifully. Today we are going to start reading the NT and see how it tells us about Jesus being there during Creation. Remember: God, Jesus, and the Holy Spirit are three in one. They are all together one God, a part of one another, but able to fulfill different roles. Let's learn some facts about the Bible before we read.

The Bible: the inspired Word of God ▶ Learn the books of the Bible to song
66 books make up one, big book
39 books in the OT, 27 books in the NT

 Please pray with your kids. Encourage them to pray also.

Scripture Memory Romans 5:6-8   Found at the beginning of this unit.

Scripture Memory Genesis 1:1-2 Have your children say this with you.

"In the beginning God created the heavens and the earth.
Now the earth was formless and empty, darkness was over the surface
of the deep, and the Spirit of God was hovering over the waters."

✓ While you read the Bible, have your kids color their sheet in their workbook.

 Bible Reading: John 1

Have the student(s) tell back what you read. Offer help along the way and kindly explain what you expect when they tell back a story. Be encouraging and compliment them.

✓ Handwriting practice

 # Science

Do you know what Science is? I am going to read you a big definition. Science is the knowledge of the systematic study of the physical and natural world through observation and experiments. What it really means is that we study and understand the world God created. It is really fun, and there is a lot we can learn!

There are people who study science who do not believe in God. Some of them have come up with some ideas that do not agree with the Bible. Do you think that's right? No, it isn't. Nothing is true if it goes against God's Word. I want you to always remember that. We can believe all of God's Word, and if something does not agree with God's Word, we know that it is not true. Another important thing to know about science is that God created the earth to function in a particular way. However, He is in charge of everything, and He can disrupt that order whenever He wants to.

What was the first thing that God did on day one of Creation? That's right! He separated the light from the darkness. We are going to study light this unit. Can you list some things that give light? It is interesting that God created light before He created the sun, moon, and stars to give light. We know that the Bible says that God IS light and in Him is no darkness at all. Darkness is often spoken of negatively in the Bible to represent sin or people who do not obey God. The Bible also tells us that Jesus is the light of the world and that no one who walks with Him walks in darkness. In Jesus is no darkness at all! Since the Bible talks so much about light this will be a very neat thing to study.

The study of light is called optics. We see light in photons and wavelengths. Light can be reflected. Can you give me an example of how light can be reflected? Think about a mirror. We can use a mirror to reflect light. Reflection of light is very important because that is how our eyes see.

Light can also be blocked and cause a shadow. Have you ever seen your shadow outside in the sun? A shadow is cast when light is blocked. The shadow will be seen on the side of the object furthest from the light. People used to tell time by shadows from the sun!

Light is a type of energy. Plants use energy from the sun as food. People also need energy from the sun. Have you ever heard of a solar panel? Solar panels receive light from the sun and use it to provide electricity. We are going to do an experiment now and answer a few questions from what we learned.

LET THERE BE LIGHT
SCIENCE ACTIVITY

We are going to do a fun experiment!

We will need:
Dark room
Flashlight
Hand-held mirror
Small toy
Piece of dark paper
Piece of light paper

After we do this activity you will record your observations and draw a picture, so pay close attention!

Please do these activities and talk about how each one is a different way that light can be reflected, blocked, partially blocked, or cast a shadow.

- Shine the flashlight at the mirror. Notice how the light reflects.
- Angle the mirror and see how the light moves.
- Stand the toy on a flat surface facing a wall. Shine the light at the toy. Notice how the toy casts a shadow. Move the light and see how the shadow moved based on the position of the light.
- Cover the flashlight with the dark paper. Notice how the light is blocked.
- Cover the flashlight with the light paper. Notice how more light is able to penetrate the light paper.

Remember that God created light. The light He made was not from a flashlight, but the concept of light is His. God once made the shadow cast by the sun go backwards! That means that He moved the sun the opposite direction that it should naturally go. God created light and He also controls it. When God sent the plagues on Egypt, He made darkness cover Egypt for three days.
Look up 2 Kings 20:8-11 and Exodus 10:21-29.

Isn't it amazing that God did not abandon His Creation but He still cares for it and is powerful over it?

 Science Activity Sheet

Practical Learning Have students repeat these facts after you.

- What state do you live in? There are 50 states in the United States.
- Do you know the name of our town or city? Do you know the name of the country we live in?
- Teach your child their address
- Teach older students to write their address
- Teach your child your phone number

Read to student:

Give time for them to answer questions and remind when needed.

Do you remember what a continent is?
How many continents are there? Can you name one of the continents?
Do you know which continent we live on?

 Language Arts Section in Student Workbook

 Observation Walk

Go on a walk outdoors and try to observe in creation what you studied in Science. Allow children to bring a notebook if they want to record their observations.
Use these three points to help start the discussion:

1 Look

Discuss what you are looking for. Find the location around your outdoor environment with the highest probability.

2 Factor

Talk about the possibilities of seeing what you studied. Is it sunny? Is it cloudy?

3 Observe

Did you find what you were looking for? Why? Why not? Did you learn something from seeing this in creation?

CHECK LIST

- ☐ Worship
- ☐ Bible Reading
- ☐ Complete worksheets with each child
- ☐ Individual reading/reading out loud
- ☐ Math of choice

WEEK 1, DAY 4

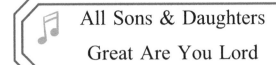

All Sons & Daughters

Great Are You Lord

Read to student:

The Bible has all different styles of writing. Some parts of the Bible are historical- they tell events that happened in the past. Some parts are prophetic- they tell/told what will/would happen in the future. There is also instruction in the Bible. That means God taught people how to live lives pleasing to Him. Another really special part of the Bible that we are going to read today is poetry and wisdom. The book of Psalms is full of songs, praises, and poems that bring glory to God. The book of Proverbs is full of wisdom! Some stories in the Bible are sad and they show a need for a Savior, Jesus. We can learn so much from the Bible! It is the best book of all time, and we know it is completely true.

Fiction: Books that are not based on a true story

Non-fiction: Books that are based on true stories or are factual

 Please pray with your kids. Encourage them to pray also.

Scripture Memory Romans 5:6-8   Found at the beginning of this unit.

Scripture Memory Genesis 1:1-2 Have your children say this with you.

"In the beginning God created the heavens and the earth.
Now the earth was formless and empty, darkness was over the surface
of the deep, and the Spirit of God was hovering over the waters."

✓ While you read the Bible, have your children color the picture on their handwriting sheet. Older children may help with the reading.

 Bible Reading: Psalm 8 and 104

Have the student(s) tell back what you read. Offer help along the way and kindly explain what you expect when they tell back a story. Be encouraging and compliment them.

✓ Handwriting Project   *Third and up write from memory.

At the end of each week have your student grades 2+ practice their best handwriting. Remove this sheet and share with a friend, family member, or persecuted/imprisoned Christian (send through Voice of the Martyrs). Have children 3rd and up address the envelope and write their return address. **NOTE: The pages for this are found at the end of your child's workbook.**

Practical Learning

Have students repeat these facts after you. Give practical examples and hands on demonstrations when possible and when needed.

- Say the Armor of God (Helmet of salvation, breastplate of righteousness, belt of truth, feet shod with the readiness of the gospel of peace, shield of faith, sword of the Spirit which is the Word of God.)
- Measurement is broken down into units. An inch is a common unit of measurement. There are 12 inches in a foot, 3 feet in a yard.

Read to student:

Give time for them to answer questions and remind when needed.

Let's review what we have learned this week.

Can you tell me something we learned from the Bible?

Do you remember what a continent is?

✓ Review anything from this week that your children struggled with. (Examples: Sight words, letters)

✓ Language Arts Section in Student Workbook

📖 Read out loud to your children. This is a great time to read historical books. Be sure to choose books that are written from a Christian perspective or audit them closely for anything that isn't God glorifying and true. Children grades 1-5 should also spend time reading age-appropriate books.

CHECK LIST

- ☐ Worship
- ☐ Bible Reading
- ☐ Complete worksheets with each child
- ☐ Individual reading/reading out loud
- ☐ Math of choice

WEEK 2, DAY 1

 God of Revival- Bethel

Read to student:

Are you excited to learn about Noah and the Ark? Can you tell me something you already know about Noah? This week will be fun! There's a lot of water involved. Do you like water? We need water to drink; it is good for us. How about swimming? Do you enjoy being in water? Jesus' first miracle involved water! Do you know what it is? We are going to learn about that this week too! Since we are learning so much about water, we are going to learn about water in science also. Do you want to know an interesting fact? Roughly 60% of our body is made up of water! That is over half. You can see why it is so important to drink water!

 Please pray with your kids. Encourage them to pray also.

Scripture Memory Romans 5:6-8

Scripture Memory Proverbs 3:5-6

"Trust in the Lord with all your heart and lean not on your own understanding; in all your ways submit to him, and he will make your paths straight."

 While you read the Bible, have your kids color the picture on their handwriting sheet.

 Bible Reading: Genesis 6-9

Have the student(s) act out the story or a portion of the story that you read. Offer help with ideas and narration. You can make this as simple or complex as you wish.

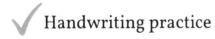 Handwriting practice

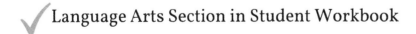 Language Arts Section in Student Workbook

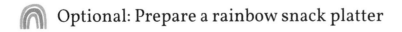 Optional: Prepare a rainbow snack platter

Review

- How many days did it take God to create the heavens and the earth?
- Can we believe everything in the Bible?
- Name one ocean.
- Name one continent.
- Did God make everything alike? How did He make each thing? (According to its kind.)
- Who is Jesus?
- Tell me one thing you are thankful for!

Read to student:

Wow! Can you imagine being on the ark for so long? What do you think that would have been like? What kind of food do you think Noah brought? What did God set in the sky as a promise never to destroy the whole earth again? What was the rainbow a sign of? (God's covenant with Noah)

Sometimes the world tries to take things of God and twist them. Satan does that with God's Word. We have to make sure we are on guard, watching for that. It is very important that we learn God's Word. We know we can believe everything in God's Word.

Do you remember how many of each animal Noah brought into the ark?

Do you notice that sometimes two of each is shown in pictures? We must read our actual Bible and rely on it for accurate information.

 Using some of the rocks you collected last week, paint Noah's Ark story rocks. Keep these- they will be used to retell the story later this week. Keep a basket of Bible story rocks (this will be added to throughout the year). For ideas and inspiration check out @Lampandlightliving on Pinterest or Instagram.

Read out loud to your children, this is a great time to read historical books. Be sure to choose books that are written from a Christian perspective or audit them closely for anything that isn't God glorifying and true. Children grades 1-5 should also spend time reading age-appropriate books.

CHECK LIST

- [ ] Worship
- [ ] Bible Reading
- [ ] Art Project
- [ ] Individual reading/reading out loud
- [ ] Complete worksheets with each child
- [ ] Math of choice

WEEK 2, DAY 2

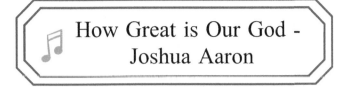
How Great is Our God - Joshua Aaron

Read to student:

Have you ever met someone who spoke a different language than you? Do you know any words in another language? Today we are learning about the Tower of Babel. This is when God confused the languages of people so we cannot all understand each other. Before this, everyone spoke the same language. Did you notice the different words in the song we listened to? Those were Hebrew. Hebrew is the language that the OT was written in.

The people after the flood decided to build a tower to heaven in order to make a name for themselves. God did not like their plan, so He confused their language. Notice that God says, "let us." Do you remember that God is three parts in one? It is so amazing how we can see this in Genesis! Sometimes when we read something called genealogies it can sound confusing. Do you know what a genealogy is? It tells the history of who someone was, who their family was, and who their parents and grandparents were. We all have genealogies. Do you know who your ancestors are? Let's name as far back in our family as we can. Genealogies in the Bible are important because they help us to know who someone is. Jesus' genealogy was especially important because He had to be from a certain family in order to be the Messiah.

 Please pray with your kids. Encourage them to pray also.

Scripture Memory Romans 5:6-8

Scripture Memory Proverbs 3:5-6

"Trust in the Lord with all your heart and lean not on your own understanding; in all your ways submit to him, and he will make your paths straight."

 While you read the Bible, have your kids color the picture on their handwriting sheet.

 Bible Reading: Genesis 10 (optional) and 11

Have the student(s) tell back what you read. Offer help along the way and kindly explain what you expect when they tell back a story. Be encouraging and compliment them.

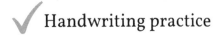 Handwriting practice

Practical Learning Have students repeat these facts after you.

- A penny is worth 1 cent, a nickel is worth 5 cents, a dime is worth 10 cents, and a quarter is worth 25 cents.
- There are 100 cents in a dollar.
- For older kids, challenge them to tell you what amount of money different combinations of coins make.

✓ Language Arts Section in Student Workbook

 Read to student:

Last week we started learning about continents. What continent do we live on? Have you visited any other continents? This week we are going to start learning about the continent of Antarctica. Antarctica is unique because it is very cold and has few people living on it. The people who do live there are primarily scientists, and less than 2,000 people live there year-round. There are no countries in Antarctica, but several countries have interests there.

We will read a book about Antarctica and work together to do some research. You will have a page to complete in your workbook.
- Have students find Antarctica on a map, globe, or in an atlas
- Read a book with basic facts about Antarctica
- Help your children research to find the information needed to complete their worksheets.

 Read out loud to your children. This is a great time to read historical books. Be sure to choose books that are written from a Christian perspective or audit them closely for anything that isn't God glorifying and true. Children grades 1-5 should also spend time reading age-appropriate books.

CHECK LIST

- ☐ Worship
- ☐ Bible Reading
- ☐ Complete worksheets with each child
- ☐ Individual reading/reading out loud
- ☐ Math of choice

WEEK 2, DAY 3

 Battler Belongs-
Phil Wickham

Read to student:

Do you enjoy reading books? Where do we usually start a new book? (Great time to show book basics) That's right. At the beginning. We started the Bible at the beginning, but sometimes we jump ahead and open the book further in without reading the whole story. The Bible is a unique book because we read it again and again, and not always in the same order. However, when we read it out of order sometimes things don't make perfect sense. For example, today we are going to read from 1 Peter. Peter was one of Jesus' disciples. You may know a little about him, but you don't know his whole story yet. Because we learned about Noah this week, and Peter mentions Noah, we are going to read from one of his letters. I want you to understand the structure of the Bible, but also to know how to find things that you need for your life and connections throughout the Word of God. We will also read from John again. John is one of the four Gospels. The Gospels tell the story of Jesus' life, ministry, death, burial, and resurrection. The Gospels are Matthew, Mark, Luke, and John. They all tell the same story of Jesus, but from a different person's perspective. It would be like if you went on a trip with me, your dad, and your siblings. We would all go together to the same places, yet we may remember different details. Let's get started!

 Please pray with your kids. Encourage them to pray also.

Scripture Memory Romans 5:6-8

Scripture Memory Proverbs 3:5-6

"Trust in the Lord with all your heart and lean not on your own understanding; in all your ways submit to him, and he will make your paths straight."

 While you read the Bible, have your kids color the picture on their handwriting sheet.

 Bible Reading: 1 Peter 3:13-22, John 2

Have the student(s) tell back what you read. Offer help along the way and kindly explain what you expect when they tell back a story. Be encouraging and compliment them.

 Handwriting practice

 # Science

Let's continue learning about light! We learned some of the ways that light operates last week. Today we are going to watch a video about light. Notice that not all light is visible. Isn't that interesting when you remember that God created light before He created the sun, moon, and stars to give light?

The color of a rainbow is the light color spectrum. Isn't that amazing?! We know that God gave Noah the rainbow as a sign of His promise. What did God promise Noah when He gave the rainbow?

▶ Watch "The Science of Light and Color for Kids: Rainbows and Electromagnetic Spectrum" from Free School on Youtube.

All videos I share I have personally audited for content to make sure that nothing is against Scripture. If you would rather teach your child this content without this video, feel free to get a book, find something on the internet, or choose your own video. You can see the basic outline of content needed by viewing your child's worksheet. Recommend to grades 3+ that they take notes during the video or fill out their worksheet while they watch.

✓ Science Worksheet and Experiment

RAINBOWS OF LIGHT
SCIENCE ACTIVITY

We are going to do a fun experiment and create a rainbow!

We will need:
- Flashlight
- Glass of water
- Piece of white paper

- Place the glass of water at the edge of the paper.
- Shine your light through the glass of water and onto the paper. Try different angels until you see a rainbow! *Some glasses work better than others.
- Record your observations on your Science Worksheet.

Practical Learning
Present these for your family without causing your kids to feel afraid. These are wise things we must teach.

- What do we do in the event of a fire? Also teach stop, drop, and roll.
- What do we do in the even of a natural disaster? Fill in with applicable events such as earthquake, tornado, other.
- Should you ever go with a stranger? NO! Even if they tell you that they know your mom and dad, you need to run and immediately come find one of your parents.

Read to student:
Give time for them to answer questions and remind when needed.

Do you remember how many days and nights it rained when Noah was on the Ark?
How many people were saved from the flood in all?
Why did God confuse the language of the people?

 Language Arts Section in Student Workbook

 Observation Walk

Go on a walk outdoors and try to <u>observe</u> in creation what you <u>studied</u> in Science. Allow children to bring a notebook if they want to record their observations.
Use these three points to help start the discussion:

1	**2**	**3**
Look	**Factor**	**Observe**
Discuss what you are looking for. Find the location around your outdoor environment with the highest probability.	Talk about the possibilities of seeing what you studied. Is it sunny? Is it cloudy? Talk about weather impacts.	Did you find what you were looking for? Why? Why not? Did you learn something from seeing this in creation?

 CHECK LIST

☐ Worship

☐ Bible Reading

☐ Complete worksheets with each child

☐ Individual reading/reading out loud

☐ Math of choice

WEEK 2, DAY 4

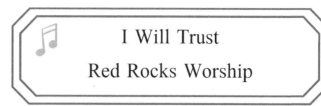
Read to student:

Today we are going to read from Proverbs. Proverbs was written by Solomon. He is the wisest person to ever live because he asked God to give him wisdom to rule God's people. Solomon wrote many proverbs. Some of them flow together, and some are one to two sentences before moving on to the next idea. Solomon knew that fearing and loving God was the most important thing. He said to trust in the LORD with all of our heart.

We can learn some very important things from Proverbs.

Did you know that Solomon was King David's son? He's the same David who defeated Goliath with a stone and sling with God's help!

 Please pray with your kids. Encourage them to pray also.

Scripture Memory Romans 5:6-8

Scripture Memory Proverbs 3:5-6

"Trust in the Lord with all your heart and lean not on your own understanding; in all your ways submit to him, and he will make your paths straight."

 While you read the Bible, have your children color the picture on their handwriting sheet. Older children may help with the reading.

 Bible Reading: Proverbs 1-3

Have the student(s) tell back what you read. Offer help along the way and kindly explain what you expect when they tell back a story. Be encouraging and compliment them.

 ## Handwriting Project   *Third and up write from memory.

At the end of each week, have your student practice their best handwriting. Remove this sheet and share with a friend, family member, or persecuted/imprisoned Christian (send through Voice of the Martyrs). Have children 3rd and up address the envelope and write their return address.

Practical Learning

Have students repeat these facts after you. Give practical examples and hands on demonstrations when possible and when needed.

- Say the fruits of the Spirit: love, joy, peace, patience, kindness, goodness, faithfulness, gentleness, and self-control.
- Weight is how we know how heavy something is. An ounce is a small unit of weight. There are 16 ounces in a pound.

Read to student:

Give time for them to answer questions and remind when needed.

Let's review what we have learned this week.

Can you tell me something we learned from the Bible?

Do you remember what a continent is?

✓ Review anything from this week that your children struggled with. (Examples: sight words, letters)

✓ Language Arts Section in Student Workbook

📖 Read out loud to your children, this is a great time to read historical books. Be sure to choose books that are written from a Christian perspective or audit them closely for anything that isn't God glorifying and true. Children grades 1-5 should also spend time reading age-appropriate books.

✓ Help your child with their worksheet and report about a historical figure.

If you have not completed a book about a historical figure, do your best to help your child find a historical person of interest to use for this exercise. Add words your child may struggle with when writing to next week's spelling list.

CHECK LIST

- ☐ Worship
- ☐ Bible Reading
- ☐ Complete worksheets with each child
- ☐ Individual reading/reading out loud
- ☐ Math of choice

WEEK 3, DAY 1

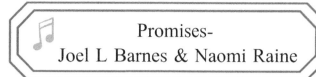
♫ Promises-
Joel L Barnes & Naomi Raine

Note to parents:

You will notice we skip lots of sections of the Bible. If you feel that it fits right with your family and study time, consider reading more than what is built into this curriculum. It is a hard decision to skip any of the Scriptures since they are all useful and good. The goal with this curriculum is to make sure that your children have a good understanding of God's Story and as much of the Bible in their little hearts and minds as they can absorb.

Read to student:

Today we meet Abram! You may have heard him called Abraham, but when we meet him in the Bible today his name is Abram. Do you know why he has two names? Yes, because God changed his name! Abraham is a VERY important person. He is called the father of all who believe. Do you know what it means to believe God? Having faith is believing God. Abraham believed God and his belief caused him to obey God. We can show our faith in God in the same way. When someone really has faith in God it is evident in the way they live their life.

 Please pray with your kids. Encourage them to pray also.

Scripture Memory Romans 5:6-8

> ### Scripture Memory James 2:23-24
>
> "And the scripture was fulfilled that says, 'Abraham believed God, and it was credited to him as righteousness,' and he was called God's friend. You see that a person is considered righteous by what they do and not by faith alone."

 While you read the Bible have your kids color the picture on their handwriting sheet.

 Bible Reading: Genesis 12:1-9, 13-15

Have the student(s) act out the story or a portion of the story that you read. Offer help with ideas and narration. You can make this as simple or complex as you wish.

 Handwriting practice

 Language Arts Section in Student Workbook

Review

- How many days did it rain when Noah was on the ark?
- How many of each animal did God send to be saved on the ark?
- What is the coldest continent?
- Tell me one thing you remember about Antarctica.
- What did Jesus turn into wine for His first public miracle?
- Do you remember your memory verse from last week?
- Tell me one thing you are thankful for!

Read to student:

Can you imagine what it would be like to have God tell you to leave your country and family? How would you feel if God asked you to do that? Would you obey?
God gave Abraham different promises throughout his life. Can you remember some of the things that God promised Abraham? What did God use to illustrate to Abraham how numerous his offspring would be?

 Today we are going to make a recipe book! It is very nice to keep all of the recipes in one place. You may make this for yourself or with the plan to gift it to someone else. We will add to it throughout the school year.

*Note to parents: This can be very basic and stapled together, or if you wish to make a nice project out of this, purchase a notebook to decorate and add to. The templates for recipes are given at the back of your student's workbook. We will also have the opportunity to add to this throughout the year when we try recipes from the countries we study.

Read out loud to your children. This is a great time to read historical books. Be sure to choose books that are written from a Christian perspective or audit them closely for anything that isn't God glorifying and true. Children grades 1-5 should also spend time reading age-appropriate books.

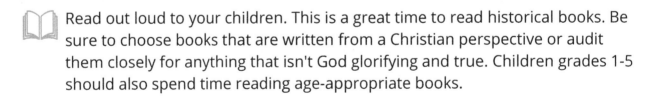

CHECK LIST

- ☐ Worship
- ☐ Bible Reading
- ☐ Art Project

- ☐ Individual reading/reading out loud
- ☐ Complete worksheets with each child
- ☐ Math of choice

WEEK 3, DAY 2

Read to student:

Do you remember who we learned about yesterday? Yes, Abraham! What did God promise Abraham? Today we are going to learn how God fulfilled His promise to Abraham. Abraham believed God for what seemed impossible. His life was not perfect because all people aside from Jesus have sinned and fallen short of God's glory. We remember Abraham as a man of great faith. He followed God, trusted God, and obeyed God. We often call God the one and only true God, the God of Abraham, Isaac, and Jacob. God gave Abraham and his sons after him a very special promise that all the nation of the earth would be blessed through them. Do you know how God did that? Jesus! Jesus is a descendant of Abraham, so they are part of the same family. Through Jesus, God's blessing to Abraham went to people of every tribe, tongue, and nation. Do you believe in Jesus? Then you are part of that family! It is a blessing to be a part of God's family. Today our reading to learn this very important story is pretty long. Before we start reading, let's sing a song to get our energy out and then we will get comfortable. SING: Father Abraham (If you do not know this song from memory look it up on YouTube and find a fun kids version to sing and do the actions with.)

 Please pray with your kids. Encourage them to pray also.

Scripture Memory Romans 5:6-8

> ### Scripture Memory James 2:23-24
>
> "And the scripture was fulfilled that says, 'Abraham believed God, and it was credited to him as righteousness,' and he was called God's friend. You see that a person is considered righteous by what they do and not by faith alone."

 While you read the Bible have your kids color the picture on their handwriting sheet. *This is a long reading so you may wish to provide a snack.

 Bible Reading: Genesis 16, 17, 18:1-15, 21:1-21, 22

Have the student(s) tell back what you read. Offer help along the way and kindly explain what you expect when they tell back a story. Be encouraging and compliment them.

 Handwriting practice

Practical Learning Have students repeat these facts after you.

- Freezing temperature of water is 32 degrees F.
- Boiling temperature of water is 212 degrees F.
- Water expands when it freezes.
- Water can be in different forms. It can be a liquid, a solid (ice), and a gas (steam).

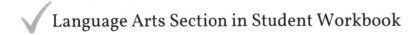 Language Arts Section in Student Workbook

 Read to student:

Today we are going to take the information we have learned about Antarctica and make it into a fun project! You will need to use your sheet from last week to put the information about Antarctica onto a poster project. When you finish this project, I am going to have you choose someone to present it to (dad, older sibling, grandparent, another family member). I want you to do your best to make this into a nice project that you feel confident sharing. Make sure you include information about Antarctica for someone who does not know anything about this continent.

*Note: You may make this a full-sized poster, or use a regular sheet of paper that can fit into a binder. We will have reports from each continent and possibly a country each month, if you and your child choose the country project that involves making a report. For our family, I intend to have a binder for each child to save these. We intend to use fun paper and make each into a scrapbook-style page, Lord willing!

Read out loud to your children. This is a great time to read historical books. Be sure to choose books that are written from a Christian perspective or audit them closely for anything that isn't God glorifying and true. Children grades 1-5 should also spend time reading age-appropriate books.

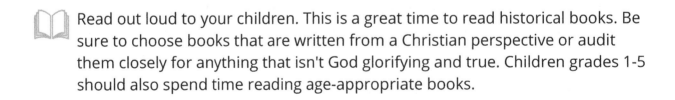

CHECK LIST

- ☐ Worship
- ☐ Bible Reading
- ☐ Complete worksheets with each child
- ☐ Individual reading/reading out loud
- ☐ Math of choice

WEEK 3, DAY 3

Throne Room-
Kim Walker-Smith

Read to student:

There are many different kinds of writing in the Bible. One of the kinds of writing we find in the NT is letters. Leaders in the faith such as Paul, Peter, James, and John wrote letters to the believers who they were discipling to follow Jesus. Today we are going to read from the letter that James wrote. I want you to notice whom he wrote to. Do you think it is encouraging to get a letter from someone you respect? Have you ever received a letter? Have you ever written a letter to encourage someone else? Today we are going to write a letter to encourage someone. I want you to think about who you could encourage and what may benefit them. You may send this letter with your Bible verse at the end of the week. If you want to share something about one of the Bible stories we have learned, that would be wonderful! Please pray about who you should send this to and ask the Lord to put a person on your heart to encourage. The Bible talks about building one another up.

*Note: Sometime over the next few days try to take a few minutes to write an encouraging note to each of your children and place it somewhere they will find it.

 Please pray with your kids. Encourage them to pray also.

Scripture Memory Romans 5:6-8

Scripture Memory James 2:23-24

"And the scripture was fulfilled that says, 'Abraham believed God, and it was credited to him as righteousness,' and he was called God's friend. You see that a person is considered righteous by what they do and not by faith alone."

 While you read the Bible, have your kids color the picture on their handwriting sheet.

 ## Bible Reading: James 1-2

Have the student(s) tell back what you read. Offer help along the way and kindly explain what you expect when they tell back a story. Be encouraging and compliment them.

 Handwriting practice

☼ Science

We were just discussing letters in Scripture. To get started on our Science lesson today I am going to read you a couple Scriptures from another letter. This letter was written by Paul to the Church in Ephesus. Read Ephesians 5:8-20.

Many times in the Bible, things from the world around us are used as pictures to make God's point. Jesus told parables, and there are word pictures all throughout Scripture to help us understand it. In Ephesians we read that light produces fruit. The light of Christ produces fruit like righteousness and truth. Did you know that light produces fruit in creation too? It does. Plants "eat" light in a process called photosynthesis. Plants need light to survive, just as we need Jesus' light to survive and bear good fruit.

Outside plants have sunshine for light. We can also grow plants indoors under special plant lights. For a plant light to work, it must provide full spectrum light. Do you remember the colors in the full spectrum of light we learned about last week? The "cool" blue end of the spectrum of light stimulates foliage and roots. Red light is needed for plants to produce flowers and fruit.

▶ Watch "Photosynthesis | Educational video for Kids" from Happy Learning English on Youtube.

✓ Science Worksheet and Experiment

☼ LEAVES BREATHE
SCIENCE ACTIVITY

We are going to do a fun experiment to show how leaves breathe oxygen out!

We will need:
- A green leaf (from outdoors or a spinach leaf)
- Bowl of water
- A window that receives light
- Submerge the leaf in the bowl of water. (You may need something to weigh this down.)
- Place in a sunny window and leave for 1 hour.
- When you return, you should see bubbles on the surface of the leaf. This is where the plant has breathed oxygen out. The water has trapped the oxygen in bubbles, so we can see it.

Practical Learning

- Each of the 50 states has a capital city. The capital of our state_____
- Washington D.C. is the capital of the United States.
- There are 12 tribes of Israel.
- Jesus had 12 disciples.

Read to student:

Give time for them to answer questions and remind when needed.

Did you notice how the beginning of James' letter is addressed to the twelve tribes in the dispersion? Some of the tribes of Israel were dispersed because they disobeyed God. We also know from the book of Acts that persecution of those who believed in Jesus caused believers to be dispersed. What are ways you can communicate with someone you don't live near?

 Language Arts Section in Student Workbook

 ## Observation Walk

Go on a walk outdoors and try to <u>observe</u> in creation what you <u>studied</u> in Science. Allow children to bring a notebook if they want to record their observations.
Use these three points to help start the discussion:

1

Look

Discuss what you are looking for. Find the location around your outdoor environment with the highest probability.

2

Factor

Talk about the possibilities of seeing what you studied. Is it the right season?

3

Observe

Did you find what you were looking for? Why? Why not? Did you learn something from seeing this in creation?

 ## CHECK LIST

- ☐ Worship
- ☐ Bible Reading
- ☐ Complete worksheets with each child
- ☐ Individual reading/reading out loud
- ☐ Math of choice

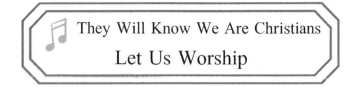
They Will Know We Are Christians
Let Us Worship

Read to student:

Psalm 105 tells some of Israel's history as a praise to God. It mentions Abraham and the covenant that God made with him. Listen to some of the people mentioned after Abraham. We will be learning more about these important men of God in the coming weeks. Romans 15:4 tells us that that everything that was written in the past was written to teach us so that through endurance and encouragement that is taught by Scripture we might have hope. We can learn so much from the people who lived before us. Their stories point to the need for a Savior, Jesus, just as our lives do. We can see how God intervenes in the lives of His people and how obedience and faith bring blessing. Let's pray that we will love God's Word!

 Please pray with your kids. Encourage them to pray also.

Scripture Memory Romans 5:6-8

> ### Scripture Memory James 2:23-24
>
> "And the scripture was fulfilled that says, 'Abraham believed God, and it was credited to him as righteousness,' and he was called God's friend. You see that a person is considered righteous by what they do and not by faith alone."

 While you read the Bible, have your children color the picture on their handwriting sheet. Older children may help with the reading.

 Bible Reading: Psalm 105

Have the student(s) tell back what you read. Offer help along the way and kindly explain what you expect when they tell back a story. Be encouraging and compliment.

 Handwriting Project   *Third and up write from memory.

At the end of each week, have your student practice their best handwriting. Remove this sheet and share with a friend, family member, or persecuted/imprisoned Christian (send through Voice of the Martyrs). Have children 3rd and up address the envelope and write their return address.

Practical Learning

Have students repeat these facts after you. Give practical examples and hands on demonstrations when possible and when needed.

- Say the Lord's Prayer.
- Volume is another way we know how much of something there is, or how much is needed. We use these often in recipes. There are 8 ounces in one cup, 2 cups in a pint, 2 pints in a quart, and 4 quarts in a gallon.

Read to student:

Give time for them to answer questions and remind when needed.

Let's review what we have learned this week.

Can you tell me something we learned from the Bible?

Do you remember what a continent is?

✓ Review anything from this week that your children struggled with. (Examples: sight words, letters)

✓ Language Arts Section in Student Workbook

📖 Read out loud to your children. This is a great time to read historical books. Be sure to choose books that are written from a Christian perspective or audit them closely for anything that isn't God glorifying and true.

✓ Spend a few minutes with each child checking in on their reading progress. Make sure older children are able to decode words in syllables. Make sure younger children are recognizing their sight words within the text of a book.

CHECK LIST

- ☐ Worship
- ☐ Bible Reading
- ☐ Complete worksheets with each child
- ☐ Individual reading/reading out loud
- ☐ Math of choice

WEEK 4, DAY 1

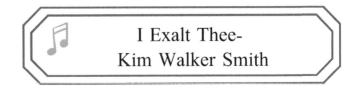

Read to student:

Are you ready for a new school week? How are you doing? Do you have anything that you need prayer for? Have you had any opportunities to tell anyone about Jesus recently? Let's pray that the Lord will give us opportunities to share the Good News of Jesus with people this week!

Throughout the rest of Scripture you will hear God called "The God of Abraham, Isaac, and Jacob," and today you are about to meet the final person in this list- Jacob! Jacob is the son of Isaac and Rebekah. He was a twin! Do you know anyone who is a twin? Twins are in their mama's belly at the same time. It is a pretty neat miracle. Jacob and Esau are the first twins we meet in Scripture. They didn't have an easy relationship. Do you ever have trouble with your siblings? There is a lot we can learn about how to treat and how not to treat our siblings. Forgiving our siblings when they do something wrong is so important! God forgives us, so we forgive others.

 Please pray with your kids. Encourage them to pray also.

Scripture Memory Romans 5:6-8

Scripture Memory Genesis 28:13b-14

"I am the Lord, the God of your father Abraham and the God of Isaac. I will give you and your descendants the land on which you are lying. Your descendants will be like the dust of the earth, and you will spread out to the west and to the east, to the north and to the south. All peoples on earth will be blessed through you and your offspring."

 While you read the Bible, have your kids color the picture on their handwriting sheet. *This is a long reading so you may wish to provide a snack.*

 Bible Reading: Genesis 24-25, 27-28

Have the student(s) act out the story or a portion of the story that you read. Offer help with ideas and narration. You can make this as simple or complex as you wish.

 Handwriting practice

 Language Arts Section in Student Workbook

Review

- What did God provide as an offering instead of Isaac?
- What is Abraham called?
- Tell me one thing you have learned this year!
- Do you remember your memory verse from last week?
- Tell me one thing you are thankful for!

Read to student:

Do you think it is nice to trick or deceive people? Has that ever happened to you? How did it make you feel? Jesus tells us that the second most important commandment is to love our neighbor as ourselves. If we love someone as we love ourselves, we treat them how we want to be treated.

Jacob tricked his father, and then he was tricked by Laban. I bet that was a very hard lesson to learn. Have you ever had to learn a lesson the hard way? God is patient with us and He allows us to learn from our mistakes. He desires that everyone would come to repentance. We need to have the humility to repent when we are wrong. We repent to God and we ask others to forgive us if we have wronged them. Do you think Jacob learned from his mistake? We will find out if he had a change of heart!

 For our art time today we are going to spend time working on our individual handicrafts. I will be available to help you if you need something. The Bible tells us to work the best we can in all we are doing. I want you to do your best work. It is good when we have skills that we are able to share with others. As we practice we get better at whatever we are working on! Don't get discouraged if you don't immediately catch on! You will get better the more you practice.

*Note to parents: Have your child work on a skill that you chose for them at the beginning of the year. It is great to have them work on this more often than is built into our curriculum, but every fourth week of our units will be a dedicated time to working on these.

 Read out loud to your children. This is a great time to read historical books. Be sure to choose books that are written from a Christian perspective or audit them closely for anything that isn't God glorifying and true. Children grades 1-5 should also spend time reading age-appropriate books.

CHECK LIST

- ☐ Worship
- ☐ Bible Reading
- ☐ Paint Story Rocks

- ☐ Individual reading/reading out loud
- ☐ Complete worksheets with each child
- ☐ Math of choice

WEEK 4, DAY 2

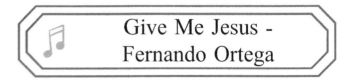

Give Me Jesus -
Fernando Ortega

Read to student:

God blessed Jacob. He prospered him and gave him many children and much livestock. Jacob lived away from his home for many years, but eventually God called him back to the Promised Land. Today we will read how Jacob handled his conflict with his brother Esau after many years of being away. Pay special attention to what God changed Jacob's name to. It is very significant. A whole nation still exists from Jacob; these are God's chosen people. God used Abraham, Isaac, Jacob, and their descendants for a special purpose. He chose them out of all the nations of the earth to be His special people. Have you heard of the Jewish people? They are descendants from Jacob's son Judah, and many live in the land of Israel. Some of them believe in Jesus as Messiah, some do not. Regardless, they have a very special and important role in God's plan and purpose. Jesus was Jewish. That means he was both an Israelite and from the tribe of Judah. One of the things the Bible tells us to do is to pray for the peace of Jerusalem. Jerusalem is a very special city in Israel where God's temple was. We will learn more about this later. For now, let's pray!

 Please pray with your kids. Encourage them to pray also.

Scripture Memory Romans 5:6-8

Scripture Memory Genesis 28:13b-14

"I am the Lord, the God of your father Abraham and the God of Isaac. I will give you and your descendants the land on which you are lying. Your descendants will be like the dust of the earth, and you will spread out to the west and to the east, to the north and to the south. All peoples on earth will be blessed through you and your offspring."

 While you read the Bible, have your kids color the picture on their handwriting sheet. *This is a long reading so you may wish to provide a snack.

 Bible Reading: Genesis 29-33, 35:1-15

Have the student(s) tell back what you read. Offer help along the way and kindly explain what you expect when they tell back a story. Be encouraging and compliment them.

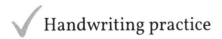 Handwriting practice

Practical Learning Have students repeat these facts after you.

- There are 5,280 feet in a mile.
- What did Jesus say the greatest commandments are? (Matt. 22:37-39)
  1. Love the LORD your God with all your heart, soul, and strength.
  2. The second is like it, love your neighbor as yourself.
     All of the Law and prophets hang on these two commands.

✓ Language Arts Section in Student Workbook

 Read to student:

Do you know how to use a map? Let's look at one! (Use a digital map or a paper map.) Maps show us things like towns. cities, streets, landmarks, rivers, lakes, and oceans. Digital maps even show you businesses! A GPS system allows you to track where you have been and to place pins so you can return to the same place.
Do you think Jacob had a map when he traveled?
An atlas is a collection of maps. They are very useful! (If you have one, spend time with your children looking at it.)

Are you familiar with direction? There are four cardinal directions. They are: north, east, south, and west. We use these to explain where places are. We also use these to tell others which way to go. The Bible talks about direction often! Direction is an important thing to grasp. The sun can help us to determine direction. The sun rises in the east and sets in the west. Can you think about where the sun rises at our house? What about where it sets? Let's see if that is east and west! (Use a compass-phone or regular.) Find N, E, S, W. Explain that the first letter of each direction capitalized is an abbreviation standing for the rest of the word.

✓ Geography Section in Student Workbook

📖 Read out loud to your children. This is a great time to read historical books. Be sure to choose books that are written from a Christian perspective or audit them closely for anything that isn't God glorifying and true. Children grades 1-5 should also spend time reading age-appropriate books.

CHECK LIST

- ☐ Worship
- ☐ Bible Reading
- ☐ Complete worksheets with each child
- ☐ Individual reading/reading out loud
- ☐ Math of choice

WEEK 4, DAY 3

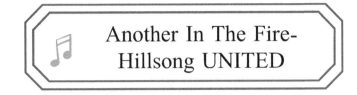
Another In The Fire-
Hillsong UNITED

Read to student:

Today we are going to read from Romans. This is another letter, this time it is written by the apostle Paul. He wrote this letter to the Church of Rome. Do you know what the Church is? It is God's people, especially when they are gathered together. It isn't a building; it is actually people. God gives different people in the Church, or the body of Christ, gifts to use to help each other. He wants us to build one another up in love. The letters in the NT were written to encourage and instruct. Isn't it neat that God preserved them for us to learn from?

One thing that is important to remember when we read from the middle of someone's letter is that there is information missing from the beginning and the end. As you get older is it important to read the letters in their entirety so you understand the full information the writers were conveying.

 Please pray with your kids. Encourage them to pray also.

Scripture Memory Romans 5:6-8

Scripture Memory Genesis 28:13b-14

"I am the Lord, the God of your father Abraham and the God of Isaac. I will give you and your descendants the land on which you are lying. Your descendants will be like the dust of the earth, and you will spread out to the west and to the east, to the north and to the south. All peoples on earth will be blessed through you and your offspring."

 While you read the Bible have your kids color the picture on their handwriting sheet.

Bible Reading: Romans 8-9, Matthew 5:14-16

Have the student(s) tell back what you read. Offer help along the way and kindly explain what you expect when they tell back a story. Be encouraging and compliment them.

 Language Arts Section in Student Workbook

💡 Science

Today we read about light in Matthew. What did Jesus say that people do with a lamp? Why don't they hide it? Yes, because then it would not fulfill its purpose to give light! Jesus also talks about a city on a hill. Have you ever seen a city built higher than the surrounding areas? Perhaps even a house that is on a hill? It is very easy to see things that are put up above what surrounds them, especially if they are lit up.

We are going to see how light is different when it is higher than its surroundings. It seems that God knew this at creation. He put the sun, moon, and stars above the earth instead of on the ground! We are supposed to live our lives for the Lord so that we are a light to others. We are supposed to do good deeds so that people will glorify God! God's word is called a lamp to our feet and a light to our path. It is both what gives light and is the light. It gives us direction to know the next step. When we walk with the LORD, we do not walk in darkness.

Isaac Newton is mentioned in today's video. Isaac Newton is a very famous historical figure. He made many incredible scientific discoveries. But, guess what? Isaac Newton wrote more words about the Bible than Science! Remember, God gives wisdom to those who fear Him and believe His words!

 **"Light for Kids | Where does light come from?" from Learn Bright on Youtube.** Some of this is review, some interesting information.

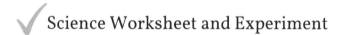 Science Worksheet and Experiment

☀ A LIGHT ON A STAND
SCIENCE ACTIVITY

Let's try a practical illustration of Scripture and put a light on a stand and under a bowl.

We will need:
- A candle and way to light it
- Some kind of stand or way to elevate the candle safely
- Glass or metal bowl
- A dark room

- Light the candle and place it on a stand. Tell your children to observe how it shines.
- Place the candle on a lower, solid surface. Tell your children to observe the difference.
- Cover the candle with the bowl, observe. *Note: if you are able to seal oxygen out and your candle goes out, use that opportunity to expand the lesson to explain that fire needs oxygen to burn.

Practical Learning

- Say the books of the Bible either from memory or with song.
- For students who are confident readers, have them do a couple Sword Drills. Sword Drills are fun competitions to see how fast you can find something in the Bible. Psalm 23:1, John 3:16, Romans 16:20

Read to student:
Give time for them to answer questions and remind when needed.

Do you feel like you live your life in a way that shines the good news of Jesus to others? What are some ways you can do that? Sometimes we have opportunities when we don't even realize it. The way we interact as a family out in public can be a light. When we speak kindly and help others, when you obey your parents, and when we are generous and friendly, we are shining the light of Jesus within us!

 Language Arts Section in Student Workbook

 Observation Walk

Go on a walk outdoors and try to <u>observe</u> in creation what you <u>studied</u> in Science. Allow children to bring a notebook if they want to record their observations.
Use these three points to help start the discussion:

1 Look

Discuss what you are looking for. Find the location around your outdoor environment with the highest probability.

2 Factor

Talk about the possibilities of seeing what you studied. Is the sun shining?

3 Observe

Did you find what you were looking for? Why? Why not? Did you learn something from seeing this in creation?

CHECK LIST

- [ ] Worship
- [ ] Bible Reading
- [ ] Complete worksheets with each child
- [ ] Individual reading/reading out loud
- [ ] Math of choice

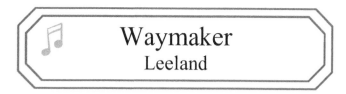
Waymaker
Leeland

Read to student:

In the Psalm we will read today, David says that the LORD is our shepherd. Do you know what shepherds do? Yes, they guard their sheep! Even in the midst of danger, a shepherd takes responsibility for his sheep and cares for them. He makes them safe and leads them to provision. What does it mean to you to have enough? Let's watch this short video about sheep in Israel.

▶ Watch "Understanding Green Pastures | Shepherd Lesson | Psalm 23" on YouTube *NOTE: Teaching given by Ray Vanderlaan

🙏 Please pray with your kids. Encourage them to pray also.

Scripture Memory Romans 5:6-8

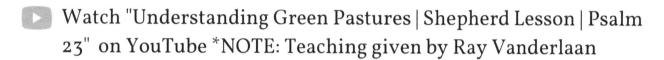

Scripture Memory Genesis 28:13b-14

"I am the Lord, the God of your father Abraham and the God of Isaac. I will give you and your descendants the land on which you are lying. Your descendants will be like the dust of the earth, and you will spread out to the west and to the east, to the north and to the south. All peoples on earth will be blessed through you and your offspring."

✓ While you read the Bible, have your children color the picture on their handwriting sheet. Older children may help with the reading.

 ## Bible Reading: Psalm 23, Proverbs 4

Have the student(s) tell back what you read. Offer help along the way and kindly explain what you expect when they tell back a story. Be encouraging and compliment them.

✓ ## Handwriting Project   *Third and up write from memory.

At the end of each week, have your student practice their best handwriting. Remove this sheet and share with a friend, family member, or persecuted/imprisoned Christian (send through Voice of the Martyrs). Have children 3rd and up address the envelope and write their return address.

End of unit review:

We are finished with our first unit of school! Wow! Great job. I am enjoying teaching you and learning with you. Let's do a review of some of the things we have learned!

Can you tell me something we learned from the Bible?

Is there one verse or lesson that really helped you?
Did the LORD comfort or convict you in any area?

What is something you learned about light?

Tell me a historical person you most enjoyed learning about. Why did you enjoy their story?

What is a continent? Tell me one thing about Antarctica.

✓ Review anything from this week that your children struggled with. (Examples: sight words, letters)

✓ Language Arts Section in Student Workbook

📖 Read out loud to your children. This is a great time to read historical books. Be sure to choose books that are written from a Christian perspective or audit them closely for anything that isn't God glorifying and true.

✓ Spend a few minutes with each child checking in on their reading progress. Make sure older children are able to decode words into syllables. Make sure younger children are recognizing their sight words within the text of a book.

CHECK LIST

☐ Worship
☐ Bible Reading
☐ Complete worksheets with each child

☐ Individual reading/reading out loud
☐ Math of choice

WEEK 5

To Parents:

The fifth week of each unit is slightly different. You and your child will be creating your own mini-unit study. This gives your child the opportunity to study something they are passionate about and wish to learn more about. This can be from a wide range of topics. You may wish to have your children take turns picking what the family will study if you are homeschooling more than one child. Often times in our family, these opportunities seem to present themselves. For example, choose a pet your family owns or wishes to own. Recently we had a bunny take up residence in our yard. We decided to welcome the bunny as a pet, which required us to learn how to take care of a bunny. This became a bit of a mini-unit study as our children learned what they need to know to own a bunny. We went on a "field trip" to the pet store to purchase the needed supplies. Another opportunity that presented itself recently was a spider that caught a bug right outside our window. We all observed the process and did some research on what was happening. Please do not be overwhelmed by this opportunity. The goal is not a strict schedule, but a fun week for you and your child to learn together and to create a love for learning. An outline is provided on the following page for you to plan. Sheets for planning are also provided in each child's workbook.
Continue Bible time by reading verses that may apply.

Examples:

If your child takes music lessons, study the history of the instrument they play.
If your child is interested in a particular sport, study the history of the sport.
A particular Bible character
A certain animal
Trains, cars, boats, airplanes, or other mechanical equipment
Flowers, trees, or insects
A person of interest, both historical or modern
A Biblical feast day or holiday (Use these weeks to pause for holiday breaks and enjoy crafts and studies related to Thanksgiving or otherwise. You are welcome to pull these weeks in at the appropriate time instead of in the fifth week of each unit. Make this work for you!)

Mini-Unit Study Plan

✓ Choose a topic

✓ Find needed resources- videos, websites, books

✓ Choose activities: field trip, experiment, movie

✓ Find Scriptures that may apply

Plan

Work with your child(ren) to come up with the best study for your family. Make a plan and allow them to be involved in finding resources and ideas.

Learn

Choose ways that learning will be involved. Examples include a write up, making lists, books to read, and more.

Enjoy

Have fun! Allow your child to talk to others about their experience. Try to enjoy this week together and foster a desire to learn more.

WEEK 5 DAILY CHECK LIST

☐ Unit Study   ☐ Math of choice

☐ Unit Study   ☐ Math of choice

☐ Unit Study   ☐ Math of choice

☐ Unit Study   ☐ Math of choice

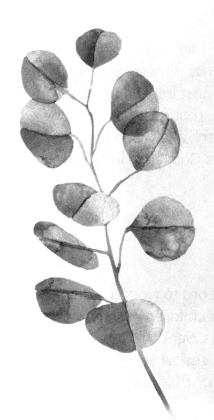

UNIT
two

GOSPEL FOCUS & EYES ON JESUS

Here's your reminder that God gave you your children. He thought you would be the best person to teach them, train them, and guide them towards Himself. We can trust the Lord to teach our children better than we ever can. Our most important job as parents is to be absolutely certain, to the best of our abilities, that our children know Jesus as Lord, and are discipled in God's ways. If you feel weary, allow God to refresh your soul. Take a few minutes to be still and know that God is God, and He will be exalted in the heavens and on the earth.

PRAY

Pause and intentionally pray over your school time. Ask the Lord to work through the time you spend educating your children to give you and your children a kingdom-first perspective. Ask the Lord to help you keep your eyes on Jesus. Seek the Lord for opportunities and ways you and your children can share the gospel and pray for anyone you have shared the gospel with. Pray for each of your children that they would know and serve the Lord.

QUESTIONS

1. Am I being intentional with our homeschool time?
2. Are we simply checking boxes or are my children learning to love Jesus and others through our schooling?
3. Do I feel burned out? If so, seek the Lord for new strength.
4. How can I best use the time I have with my children? Are we too busy to focus on what matters most?
5. Have I let distractions creep into our day that we need to reduce?

EXTRA
Resources

UNIT VERSE

Say this verse when prompted with your kids. The goal with this verse is not perfect memorization in younger grades. The goal is Scripture truth being on their heart and mind.

*Aim for weekly memory verses to be quoted by each child and written from memory for grades 4-5.

"Then Jesus came to them and said, 'All authority in heaven and on earth has been given to me. Therefore go and make disciples of all nations, baptizing them in the name of the Father and of the Son and of the Holy Spirit, and teaching them to obey everything I have commanded you. And surely I am with you always, to the very end of the age.'"

Matthew 28:18-20

PRAYER REQUESTS

Record things you and your children would like to pray over here. Be sure to check back and praise the Lord when He answers. Prompt your kids to think about praying for others. Read Matthew 6:9-13 for how Jesus taught us to pray. As you study the Word, notice the pattern of Biblical prayers and prayer requests and try to learn from the Word.

_____   _____

_____   _____

_____   _____

_____   _____

_____   _____

WEEK 1, DAY 1

Read to student:

Today we are starting our second unit of the year! Are you excited? We have so many amazing things to learn and we get to hide more Scripture in our hearts. We have a new unit verse, a new continent to study, and a new science concept to learn about. We are going to start this unit by learning about Joseph. Do you know anything about Joseph? The continent we will be studying is Africa. Did you know that Egypt, where Joseph was sold, is in Africa? Isn't that neat?

Do you remember what God created on day 2? Yes, the separation between the waters above and the water below. In this unit, we will learn about water, the cycle between the earth and the sky, clouds, and more. Water is a very essential part of life! Over half of our body is water! And over half of the earth is covered by water. It seems pretty important, right? A person can only live for 3 days without water. It is a very essential and needed part of life. No wonder Jesus calls Himself living water! We know that Jesus is just as essential to our lives as real water. I am so thankful for water to drink and for Jesus, the Living Water.

Let's get started on Unit 2!

 Please pray with your kids. Encourage them to pray also.

Scripture Memory Matthew 28:18-20

> ### Scripture Memory Genesis 50:20 Have your children say this with you.
>
> "You intended to harm me, but God intended it for good to accomplish what is now being done, the saving of many lives."

 While you read the Bible, have your kids color their sheet in their workbook.

 📖 Bible Reading: Genesis 37,39-41

Have the student(s) tell back what you read. Offer help along the way and kindly explain what you expect when they tell back a story. Be encouraging and compliment them.

 Handwriting practice

Review

- Say the ABCs
- (1st +) Do you remember what nouns and verbs are? (Noun- person, place, or thing. Verb- a word that shows action.)
- (1st +) When do we capitalize the first letter of a word? (Beginning of a sentence, proper noun, and the word I.)
- We are going to learn (practice) the calendar. Do you know many days are in a week? How many months are in a year?
  Say the days of the week and the months of the year.

 Language Arts Section in Student Workbook

Read to student:

Throughout Joseph's life, God was with him. God did not leave him even when he was in Egypt, even when he was thrown into prison! God was with Joseph. He had a plan for Joseph's life even when it seemed like everything went wrong. Have you ever had a season that was really difficult? Have you noticed that God can work even in difficult times in our life? Later on this week we are going to read a Psalm about God being our Protector. I am going to read you one verse of that Psalm right now so you will understand why we are making this art project. I want you to think about someone who may need a reminder that God is faithful and is with them. You can give this key chain to them as a gift and a reminder to them. Please read Psalm 91:4. *At the end of this week, your child's workbook has a notecard to gift with this verse attached to their weekly verse sheet.

 Make a feather key chain with your child. See Lamp & Light Living Unit 2 Pinterest board for leather and macramé key chain ideas. If this does not interest you, find a similar handicraft to work on with your child. Encourage your child to do their best work to give to someone else as a blessing.

 Read out loud to your children. This is a great time to read historical books. Be sure to choose books that are written from a Christian perspective or audit them closely for anything that isn't God-glorifying and true. Children grades 1-5 should also spend time reading age-appropriate books.

CHECK LIST

- [ ] Worship
- [ ] Bible Reading
- [ ] Art Project

- [ ] Individual reading/reading out loud
- [ ] Complete worksheets with each child
- [ ] Math of choice

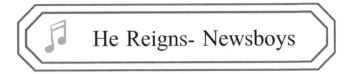

Read to student:

Joseph lived in Egypt for a long time. Do you think it was hard for him to keep believing the dreams that God had given him when he was younger? Joseph must have felt forgotten at times, yet he kept his faith in God.

Today we are going to learn the rest of Joseph's story and how God's chosen people ended up in Egypt. We are going to learn that often God tells people things that are going to happen before they happen. Sometimes He uses dreams and sometimes He uses visions or prophecy. We should not despise the things that God speaks through. We should desire to know God and to be in His presence. We should eagerly desire for God to speak to us. When we are around people who love and obey God, we can also listen to what God speaks through them. It is wise to walk by the Holy Spirit. God knows everything that happens before it happens. Just as God helped Joseph to save many people, so He can use people now to prepare others for things that are to come. We will learn more about how God speaks as we continue to read God's Word.

 Please pray with your kids. Encourage them to pray also.

Scripture Memory Matthew 28:18-20

Scripture Memory Genesis 50:20 Have your children say this with you.

"You intended to harm me, but God intended it for good to accomplish what is now being done, the saving of many lives."

 While you read the Bible, have your kids color their sheet in their workbook.

 Bible Reading: Genesis 42-46:7, 47:1-12, 49:29-33, 50

Have the student(s) tell back what you read. Offer help along the way and kindly explain what you expect when they tell back a story. Be encouraging and compliment them.

 Handwriting practice

Practical Learning Have students repeat these facts after you.

- There are 24 hours in a day, 60 minutes in an hour, and 60 seconds in a minute.
- There are 52 weeks in a year and 7 days in a week.
- "Thirty days hath September, April, June, and November; all the rest have 31 except February which has 28, except in a leap year when it has 29."
- There are 365 days in a year. A leap year has 366.

✓ Language Arts Section in Student Workbook

 Look at a globe or map with your child. Show them Africa. Point out different countries in Africa and ask them to begin thinking about which country they would like to study more.

Read to student:

Today we are going to begin learning about Africa. Africa is mentioned in the Bible several times. The queen of Ethiopia came to visit Solomon because of his wisdom from God. Ethiopia is still a country is Africa! Egypt is in Africa, although it is often thought of as a middle eastern country, it is technically in Africa. It is the second largest continent both in size and population, following Asia in both categories. There are 54 countries in Africa and more than 1.3 billion people live there! Wow! There is a rich missions history in Africa and a significant number of our brothers and sisters in Christ live in Africa!

 Read a continent book about Africa.

✓ Continent Study in Student Workbook

 Read out loud to your children. This is a great time to read historical books. Be sure to choose books that are written from a Christian perspective or audit them closely for anything that isn't God-glorifying and true. Children grades 1-5 should also spend time reading age-appropriate books.

CHECK LIST

- ☐ Worship
- ☐ Bible Reading
- ☐ Complete worksheets with each child
- ☐ Individual reading/reading out loud
- ☐ Math of choice

 WEEK 1, DAY 3

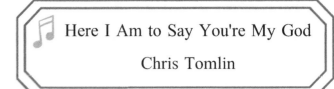
Here I Am to Say You're My God

Chris Tomlin

Read to student:

Have you heard of a parable? A parable is a short story used to teach an important point. They may, or may not, have really happened. These are passed down through generations to remember something very important. Jesus often taught using parables. These stories help us to remember the truth that Jesus taught that He wanted his disciples to remember. Jesus also used physical things to teach spiritual truth and realities. We have already talked about how Jesus is light. Today we will read how Jesus is also living water. Jesus got thirsty just like you and me for the kind of water we are going to learn about today- H20. But He also said that everyone who drinks water from the earth will be thirsty again. Spiritually we must drink from Jesus and have a spring of water within us that wells up to eternal life.

Do you remember when Jesus changed water- H20- into wine? There are so many incredible miracles God did that involve water in the Bible. Let's think of other examples! (Water from a rock, parting of the Jordan River or the Red Sea)

The Bible: the inspired Word of God ▶ Learn the books of the Bible to song

66 books make up one, big book

39 books in the OT, 27 books in the NT

 Please pray with your kids. Encourage them to pray also.

Scripture Memory Matthew 28:18-20

Scripture Memory Genesis 50:20 Have your children say this with you.

"You intended to harm me, but God intended it for good to accomplish what is now being done, the saving of many lives."

 While you read the Bible, have your kids color their sheet in their workbook.

 Bible Reading: Matthew 18, John 3

Have the student(s) tell back what you read. Offer help along the way and kindly explain what you expect when they tell back a story. Be encouraging and compliment them.

 Handwriting practice

Science

Today we are going to learn about water. On the second day of creation, God separated the water below from the water above. Water is essential for life!
The Bible has so many stories about water. What miracle did we already learn about Jesus and water?
When there is deficient rainfall, and therefore not enough water, this is a drought. God used droughts to get the attention of His people. Elijah prayed that it would not rain in Israel and God answered his prayer. He prayed again and God sent rain. We know that God created water and He still controls water. Before we start our video, we are going to get a glass of water and some ice to check out water in its different forms.

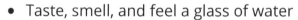

H2O
SCIENCE ACTIVITY

We will need:
- Ice
- A bowl
- A glass of water for each child
- A way to boil water and observe steam

- Taste, smell, and feel a glass of water
- Observe the difference between water in its liquid, solid, and gas state
- How long did it take for the ice to start melting? Does it taste and smell the same?

The goal of this activity is to allow your child to see water in each of its forms and to experience its similarities and differences.

 Watch "Water Water Everywhere" from Learn Bright on Youtube.

 Science Worksheet

Practical Learning

Present these to your family without causing your kids to feel afraid. These are wise things we must teach.

- What do we do in the event of a fire? *Also teach stop, drop, and roll
- What do we do in the event of a natural disaster *fill in with applicable events such as earthquake, tornado, other.
- Should you ever go with a stranger? NO! Even if they tell you that they know your mom and dad, you need to run and immediately go find one of your parents.

 Language Arts Section in Student Workbook

 Observation Walk

Go on a walk outdoors and try to <u>observe</u> in creation what you <u>studied</u> in Science. Allow children to bring a notebook if they want to record their observations.
Use these three points to help start the discussion:

1

Look

Discuss what you are looking for. Find the location around your outdoor environment with the highest probability.

2

Factor

Talk about the possibilities of seeing what you studied. Do you have a creek nearby?
What state might you see water in?

3

Observe

Did you find what you were looking for? Why? Why not? Did you learn something from seeing this in creation?

CHECK LIST

- [ ] Worship
- [ ] Bible Reading
- [ ] Complete worksheets with each child
- [ ] Individual reading/reading out loud
- [ ] Math of choice

 WEEK 1, DAY 4

Protector

Kim Walker Smith

Read to student:

Psalm 91 is a beautiful Psalm of confidence in the protection we have in God. He is our refuge. We have shelter in the Almighty. He commands His angels concerning us. When we call on God, He answers.

Earlier this week we read the verse about God covering us with His feathers and finding refuge under His wings. When God is literally described in the Bible He does not have wings or feathers so we can be fairly confident this is a word picture. Mother birds cover their babies under their wings to protect them and shelter them. In the same way, God cares for us. We can draw near to Him and expect to find care and shelter from God. When you do your handwriting today, you may cut this verse out to gift with the project you made earlier this week.

 Please pray with your kids. Encourage them to pray also.

Scripture Memory Matthew 28:18-20

Scripture Memory Genesis 50:20   Have your children say this with you.

"You intended to harm me, but God intended it for good to accomplish what is now being done, the saving of many lives."

 While you read the Bible, have your children color the picture on their handwriting sheet. Older children may help with the reading.

 Bible Reading: Psalm 91, Proverbs 10

Have the student(s) tell back what you read. Offer help along the way and kindly explain what you expect when they tell back a story. Be encouraging and compliment them.

 Handwriting Project   *Third and up write from memory.

At the end of each week, have your student practice their best handwriting. Remove this sheet and share with a friend, family member, or persecuted/imprisoned Christian (send through Voice of the Martyrs). Have children 3rd and up address the envelope and write their return address.

Practical Learning

Have students repeat these facts after you. *Give practical examples and hands on demonstrations when possible and when needed.

- Say the Armor of God (Helmet of salvation, the breastplate of righteousness, the belt of truth, feet shod with the readiness of the gospel of peace, shield of faith, sword of the Spirit which is the Word of God.)
- Measurement is broken down into units. An inch is a common unit of measurement. There are 12 inches in a foot and 3 feet in a yard.

Read to student:

Give time for them to answer questions and remind them when needed.

Let's review what we have learned this week.

Can you tell me something we learned from the Bible?

Tell me something we learned about Africa.

How many countries are in Africa?

✓ Review anything from this week that your children struggled with. (Examples: Sight words, letters)

✓ Language Arts Section in Student Workbook

📖 Read out loud to your children. This is a great time to read historical books. Be sure to choose books that are written from a Christian perspective or audit them closely for anything that isn't God-glorifying and true. Children grades 1-5 should also spend time reading age-appropriate books.

CHECK LIST

- ☐ Worship
- ☐ Bible Reading
- ☐ Complete worksheets with each child
- ☐ Individual reading/reading out loud
- ☐ Math of choice

 # WEEK 2, DAY 1

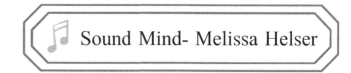 Sound Mind- Melissa Helser

Read to student:

Today we are going to start learning a very important and awesome story! Are you ready? Do you have any guesses on what we are going to learn? We are going to learn about Moses and the exodus of God's people from slavery in Egypt. Do you remember how God's people went to Egypt because of the famine? Well, that was a wonderful thing; however, eventually, the Egyptians forgot Joseph, and they made his family slaves. We are going to learn about that today. God never forgot His people and He heard their cry. Have you ever had a hard time? Do you remember to pray and ask God for help? That is the best thing we can do when we are struggling! God always hears our prayers. God heard His people (we call them the Israelites or Hebrews). He heard their prayers and cries for help and He sent Moses to bring them out of slavery.

 Please pray with your kids. Encourage them to pray also.

Scripture Memory Matthew 28:18-20

> ### Scripture Memory Psalm 37:7   Have your children say this with you.
>
> "Be still before the Lord and wait patiently for him;
> do not fret when people succeed in their ways,
> when they carry out their wicked schemes."

 While you read the Bible, have your kids color the picture on their handwriting sheet.

 Bible Reading: Exodus 1-3

Have the student(s) act out the story or a portion of the story that you read. Offer help with ideas and narration. You can make this as simple or complex as you wish.

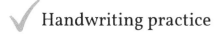 Handwriting practice

Language Arts Section in Student Workbook

Review + Focus

- What continent did we study in our last unit? Tell me one fact about it!
- How would you share the gospel with someone? Start with telling them who Jesus is. (Help as needed, encourage your kids to use what they practice to really share about Jesus with kids they encounter in your neighborhood, at the park, or otherwise.)
- Tell me one prayer that God has answered for you!
- Tell me one thing you are thankful for!

Read to student:

Can you imagine being Moses? What would it be like to have to move away from your country? Moses knew he was a Hebrew yet he looked like an Egyptian. He was no longer welcome in Egypt, so he spent a long time in Midian. Do you think he thought that God had forgotten him? What would it be like to have God appear to you in a burning bush? Wow! What did God tell Moses to do when he called to him from the bush? Yes, he told him to take his sandals off. Do you remember how God told Moses His name? The name of God is YHWH. Do you know how we have talked about words always needing to have a vowel? Well, YHWH does not have any vowels. That makes it almost impossible to pronounce! There are people who have tried the best they can to discover the vowels. In most translations of the Bible, you will see either the LORD or Jehovah for the name of the one, true God we worship. It is important that we know the name of God. He is not just any god. There are false gods, but we serve the one, true, powerful, Almighty God who created everything! He is not just a god, He is the only real God!

Do you remember what Moses' mother put him in to save him from Pharaoh? Yes! A basket. Today for our art project we are going to begin making a basket.

 For ideas and inspiration check out @Lampandlightliving on Pinterest or Instagram. You can choose any style of DIY basket to make with your children.

 Read out loud to your children. This is a great time to read historical books. Be sure to choose books that are written from a Christian perspective or audit them closely for anything that isn't God-glorifying and true. Children grades 1-5 should also spend time reading age-appropriate books.

CHECK LIST

- [ ] Worship
- [ ] Bible Reading
- [ ] Paint Story Rocks
- [ ] Individual reading/reading out loud
- [ ] Complete worksheets with each child
- [ ] Math of choice

WEEK 2, DAY 2

Read to student:

We are going to pick back up with Moses and God speaking to him. Can you "set the stage" for where this conversation was taking place? Once Moses got to Egypt, God sent the 10 plagues on Egypt to show Himself as the true God and the Deliverer of His people. We are going to learn more about this during Passover. For now, what is important for us to know is that God went with Moses, God showed His power, and He delivered His people with mighty signs and wonders! He destroyed the country of Egypt and many of the Egyptians. Opposing God is never a good idea!

Next week we will learn about the people of Israel in the desert. When they left Egypt they had to journey through the desert. Do you think God left them in the desert? No! Of course not. He helped them and went with them.

*Read Exodus 14:31 at the end of the Bible reading time as a bit of a summary of the events that we skip.

 Please pray with your kids. Encourage them to pray also.

Scripture Memory Matthew 28:18-20

> ### Scripture Memory Psalm 37:7   Have your children say this with you.
>
> "Be still before the Lord and wait patiently for him;
> do not fret when people succeed in their ways,
> when they carry out their wicked schemes."

 While you read the Bible, have your kids color the picture on their handwriting sheet.

 Bible Reading: Exodus 4-6:13, 6:28-7:13, 12:31-33, 14:31

Have the student(s) tell back what you read. Offer help along the way and kindly explain what you expect when they tell back a story. Be encouraging and compliment them.

 Handwriting practice

Practical Learning
Have students repeat these facts after you.

- A penny is worth 1 cent, a nickel is worth 5 cents, a dime is worth 10 cents, and a quarter is worth 25 cents.
- There are 100 cents in a dollar.
- For older kids, challenge them to tell you what amount of money different combinations of coins makes.

 Language Arts Section in Student Workbook

 Read to student:

Do you remember what you learned last week about Africa? Today we are going to have some fun with what we learned! We are going to make the information you learned into a visual report that you can share with others. There is a sheet in your workbook to help you get started. *For inspiration check the Unit 2 Pinterest board from @lampandlightliving.

Things to consider encouraging your child to add:
- Visual appeal with colors, themes, and facts
- Stickers, printed or magazine images, or drawings
- Number of countries
- Top natural resources
- Main religion, percent of known Christians *Be sure to share that this isn't always accurate if a country has laws against Christianity. We could have brothers and sisters in Christ not openly declaring their religion.
- Main bodies of water
- Any significant landmarks, both natural and man-made

Read out loud to your children. This is a great time to read historical books. Be sure to choose books that are written from a Christian perspective or audit them closely for anything that isn't God-glorifying and true. Children grades 1-5 should also spend time reading age-appropriate books.

 CHECK LIST

- [ ] Worship
- [ ] Bible Reading
- [ ] Complete worksheets with each child
- [ ] Individual reading/reading out loud
- [ ] Math of choice

 WEEK 2, DAY 3

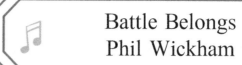
Battle Belongs
Phil Wickham

Read to student:

What do you think it means that God's thoughts are higher than our thoughts? In Isaiah 55 we read that God's thoughts are higher than our thoughts and His ways are higher than our ways. In times when we don't understand God's ways, we can think about seeds.

Just as rain causes seeds to grow and sprout, leading to a harvest, so it is with God. What He speaks has a purpose. His commands and ways lead to a harvest even when we do not always understand how or why. We can trust and obey Him because we know that He is faithful. We know that His Words cause growth and that they accomplish their purpose.

 Please pray with your kids. Encourage them to pray also.

Scripture Memory Matthew 28:18-20

Scripture Memory Psalm 37:7   Have your children say this with you.

"Be still before the Lord and wait patiently for him;
do not fret when people succeed in their ways,
when they carry out their wicked schemes."

 While you read the Bible, have your kids color the picture on their handwriting sheet.

 Bible Reading: John 4, Isaiah 55

Have the student(s) tell back what you read. Offer help along the way and kindly explain what you expect when they tell back a story. Be encouraging and compliment them.

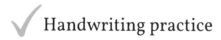 Handwriting practice

Science

Do you remember what H2O is? Yes! You're right! Water! When we read today about Jesus, what did He say about water? He said that He offers living water. He also said that everyone who drinks water from the earth will get thirsty again. In Isaiah 55, Isaiah talks about the water cycle and compares it to the Word of God. We know that Jesus is the living Word of God. Isn't that neat? Jesus, God's Word, never returns empty. He was and is always accomplishing God's purposes on the earth just as water is always causing seeds to grow into plants!

Did you know that you can only live for 3 days without water? That is not very long. Water is so important!

A well (like Jesus was at) is dug or drilled into the ground to get fresh water. Did you know that there is water underground? When God flooded the earth during Noah's time the Bible says that the waters of the deep broke open. Perhaps these underground rivers are what God was talking about! Today we are going to learn about the water cycle. The water cycle is a very important part of life. God made such a neat and perfect system. Remember that He is in control of it at every step and He can disrupt the water cycle anytime He wants to! Understanding the water cycle will help us to understand and appreciate weather and fresh water!

▶ Watch "All About the Water Cycle for Kids" from Free School on Youtube.

✓ Science Worksheet and Experiment

 ## MAKE IT RAIN
SCIENCE ACTIVITY

We are going to do a fun experiment and create "rain"!

We will need:
- Large bowl with water
- Empty cup or mug
- Saran Wrap (tape or rubber band to hold securely in place)

- Put the mug or cup in the bowl of water
- Cover tightly with Saran wrap
- Place in a warm, sunny area for a few hours
- Check back and see condensation "rain" that formed on the Saran wrap and fell into the empty cup. Relate to the water cycle process and have your child explain each part.

Practical Learning
Present these for your family and without causing your kids to feel afraid. They are wise things we must teach.

- What do we do in the event of a fire? *Also teach stop, drop, and roll
- What do we do in the event of a natural disaster? *fill in with applicable events such as earthquakes, tornadoes, or other.
- Should you ever go with a stranger? NO! Even if they tell you that they know your mom and dad you need to run and immediately come to find one of your parents.

 Language Arts Section in Student Workbook

 ## Observation Walk

Go on a walk outdoors and try to <u>observe</u> in creation what you <u>studied</u> in Science. Allow children to bring a notebook if they want to record their observations.
Use these three points to help start the discussion:

1	2	3
Look	**Factor**	**Observe**
Discuss what you are looking for. Find the location around your outdoor environment with the highest probability.	Talk about the possibilities of seeing what you studied. Is it sunny? Is it cloudy? Talk the water cycle in creation.	Did you find what you were looking for? Why? Why not? Did you learn something from seeing this in creation?

 ## CHECK LIST

- ☐ Worship
- ☐ Bible Reading
- ☐ Complete worksheets with each child
- ☐ Individual reading/reading out loud
- ☐ Math of choice

 WEEK 2, DAY 4

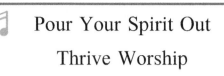
♪ Pour Your Spirit Out
Thrive Worship

Read to student:

Have you ever felt like someone did something bad and they got away with it? Do you think the Israelites felt like that when they were slaves in Egypt? Today we are going to read Psalm 37. It has so many beautiful reminders. When Jesus met the woman at the well He knew everything she had ever done. Jesus extends mercy and grace when we repent for the bad things we have done. How God redeems us is our testimony! God can take anyone who is willing to turn their heart towards Him and bring change and beautiful testimony of His greatness to our life. We want to be like the woman at the well, not like Pharaoh who hardened his heart against God. Let's pray that we will have soft hearts toward God and the opportunity to share our testimony of God's greatness with others!

 Please pray with your kids. Encourage them to pray also.

Scripture Memory Matthew 28:18-20

Scripture Memory Psalm 37:7   Have your children say this with you.

"Be still before the Lord and wait patiently for him;
do not fret when people succeed in their ways,
when they carry out their wicked schemes."

 While you read the Bible, have your children color the picture on their handwriting sheet. Older children may help with the reading.

 Bible Reading: Psalm 37

Have the student(s) tell back what you read. Offer help along the way and kindly explain what you expect when they tell back a story. Be encouraging and compliment them.

 Handwriting Project   *Third and up write from memory.

At the end of each week, have your student practice their best handwriting. Remove this sheet and share with a friend, family member, or persecuted/imprisoned Christian (send through Voice of the Martyrs). Have children 3rd and up address the envelope and write their return address.

Practical Learning

Have students repeat these facts after you. *Give practical examples and hands-on demonstrations when possible and when needed.

- Say the fruits of the Spirit: love, joy, peace, patience, kindness, goodness, faithfulness, gentleness, and self-control.
- Weight is how we know how heavy something is. An ounce is a small unit of weight. There are 16 ounces in a pound.

Read to student:

Give time for them to answer questions and remind them when needed.

Let's review what we have learned this week.

Can you tell me something we learned from the Bible?

Tell me one fact about Africa.

✓ Review anything from this week that your children struggled with. (Examples: sight words, letters)

✓ Language Arts Section in Student Workbook

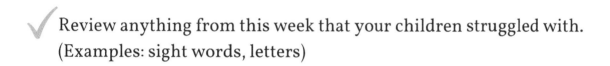 Read out loud to your children. This is a great time to read historical books. Be sure to choose books that are written from a Christian perspective or audit them closely for anything that isn't God-glorifying and true. Children grades 1-5 should also spend time reading age-appropriate books.

✓ Help your child with their worksheet and report about a historical figure.

If you have not completed a book about a historical figure, do your best to help your child find a historical person of interest to use for this exercise. Add words that your child may struggle with when writing to next week's spelling list.

CHECK LIST

- ☐ Worship
- ☐ Bible Reading
- ☐ Complete worksheets with each child
- ☐ Individual reading/reading out loud
- ☐ Math of choice

WEEK 3, DAY 1

Read to student:

What are some of the rules we have at our house? Why do we have rules? Sometimes it can seem like they keep us from doing the things we want to do, but usually, they are for our safety, the safety of others, and the overall functioning of society and our homes. When God brought His people out of Egypt, He was essentially starting fresh. He had rules that He needed to give to His people to teach them the best way to live. He wanted them to have a blessing and a relationship with Him. We call the rules that God gave "The Law" or "The Torah." Are you familiar with the 10 Commandments? They are a part of the Law. God gave them to Moses written on stone tablets. Jesus said the greatest commandments are to love the LORD our God with all of our heart, soul, and strength and to love our neighbor as ourselves. Many people believe the 10 Commandments tell us how to do that, along with the rest of the Law. Jesus said that all of the Law and the Prophets hang on those two commands.

 Please pray with your kids. Encourage them to pray also.

Scripture Memory Matthew 28:18-20

Scripture Memory Matthew 22:37-38   Have your children say this with you.

Jesus replied: "'Love the Lord your God with all your heart and with all your soul and with all your mind.' This is the first and greatest commandment. And the second is like it: 'Love your neighbor as yourself.' "

 While you read the Bible, have your kids color the picture on their handwriting sheet.

 Bible Reading: Exodus 19-20

Have the student(s) act out the story or a portion of the story that you read. Offer help with ideas and narration. You can make this as simple or complex as you wish.

 Handwriting practice

 Language Arts Section in Student Workbook

Review

- How many days did it take God to create the world?
- How many of each animal did God send to be saved on the ark?
- Tell me the continents we have studied so far.
- What did Jesus turn into wine for His first public miracle?
- Do you remember your memory verse from last week?
- How did God save Moses?
- Tell me one thing you are thankful for!

Read to student:

Can you imagine what it would have been like to be at Mount Sinai? Do you think you would have been afraid? Why were the people afraid? God said that the people were not to make any image to represent Him. What was His reason for this commandment? Do you feel that we follow the 10 Commandments? Where can we improve? God is the same, yesterday, today, and forever. We want to learn how to honor Him and obey Him. Jesus forgives us for our sins, but we do not want to go on sinning. The Law defines what sin is (1 John 3:4).

 Our art project for today is to make a holder for Bible verses. We can use this to display different Bible verses, you may add your own beyond the ones provided if you want. This is a great thing to add to throughout the year and you can make a second one to gift if desired! NOTE: Bible verse cards for this are found at the back of your child's workbook.

Please visit @lampandlightliving on Pinterest and view the board "Unit 2" for ideas for the rock & wire holder.

 Read out loud to your children. This is a great time to read historical books. Be sure to choose books that are written from a Christian perspective or audit them closely for anything that isn't God-glorifying and true. Children grades 1-5 should also spend time reading age-appropriate books.

CHECK LIST

- ☐ Worship
- ☐ Bible Reading
- ☐ Art Project

- ☐ Individual reading/reading out loud
- ☐ Complete worksheets with each child
- ☐ Math of choice

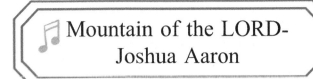
♫ Mountain of the LORD-
Joshua Aaron

Read to student:

Deuteronomy was recorded at the end of Moses' life. It is his final reminder to the Israelites. The whole book is so good! It is a great reminder to parents to teach God's ways to their children. It is always important for us to remember what God has done and what He has taught us. We must remember to tell the next generation about God and His faithfulness. Someday you will be the parent! I want to make sure I do my best so that you will be well equipped to pass these things on to your children. The Bible talks about having a heritage of those who fear the LORD. I am thankful that you have that. If you continue to follow in God's ways, your children will have that too! When we remember to obey God and to acknowledge Him in all we do, it is a blessing for us and those after us! Moses really, really wanted the people to walk in God's ways. He knew how sad and terrible it would be for them if they didn't. God is so kind and He gave them a way out of bad decisions if they failed to obey. Later in the book of Deuteronomy, Moses tells the people a list of blessings for obeying and curses for disobeying. He tells them that if they disobeyed and all the curses came upon them, they just had to repent and turn back to the LORD, and the LORD would be merciful to them. And that is exactly what happened!

 Please pray with your kids. Encourage them to pray also.

Scripture Memory Matthew 28:18-20

Scripture Memory Matthew 22:37-38   Have your children say this with you.

Jesus replied: "'Love the Lord your God with all your heart and with all your soul and with all your mind.' This is the first and greatest commandment. And the second is like it: 'Love your neighbor as yourself.' "

✓ While you read the Bible, have your kids color the picture on their handwriting sheet.

📖 Bible Reading: Deuteronomy 4-6, 8

Have the student(s) tell back what you read. Offer help along the way and kindly explain what you expect when they tell back a story. Be encouraging and compliment them.

 Handwriting practice

Practical Learning Have students repeat these facts after you.

- Freezing temperature of water is 32 degrees F.
- Boiling temperature of water is 212 degrees F.
- Water expands when it freezes.
- Water can be in different forms. It can be a liquid, a solid (ice), and a gas (steam).

 Language Arts Section in Student Workbook

 Read to student:

Today is our first country study! We are going to study one country from the continent of Africa. If you have not already done so, please choose a country on the continent of Africa to study. We are going to work together to find the answers to the questions on your worksheet. Next week we will choose a project to do for the country you chose. You will have different options to choose from. You may look ahead in your book now and decide which project you will do. While we study, we will look for information to prepare for next week.

Every country is unique. They have distinct features both geographically and culturally. Some countries are very diverse. Take the United States for example. There are different areas of the United States that have very different cultures. How we talk even sounds a little bit different! There are certain areas that have unique styles of food, the climate varies, and the natural resources and job opportunities vary. While there is variation within a country, a country shares a common government, currency (money), main language, and laws.

 Read out loud to your children. This is a great time to read historical books. Be sure to choose books that are written from a Christian perspective or audit them closely for anything that isn't God-glorifying and true. Children grades 1-5 should also spend time reading age-appropriate books.

CHECK LIST

- ☐ Worship
- ☐ Bible Reading
- ☐ Complete worksheets with each child
- ☐ Individual reading/reading out loud
- ☐ Math of choice

WEEK 3, DAY 3

Throne Room
Kim Walker-Smith

Read to student:

The Sermon on the Mount, as we call it, is the longest recorded discourse/teaching of Jesus. It is found in Matthew 5-7 and is full of wisdom. Much of it is dedicated to explaining what the people had heard said and taught by their teachers. Jesus explained everything perfectly. He is the greatest teacher ever. He is the Word made flesh, fully God and fully man. He was able to explain the intent behind the commandments perfectly because He is the one who wrote them. He came to live it out exactly and to teach it to others. Throughout the Sermon on the Mount, Jesus quotes from the Law and teaches about our hearts being as important as our actions. He explained how what is inside of a person matters. Out of the heart comes bad things if there is bad inside of us. If we have good in our hearts we will produce good motives and good actions. We must seek to please God in how we live and think!

*Note: There is a video of the Sermon on the Mount being read/acted out with visuals. You may wish to watch that for Matthew 5-7.

 Please pray with your kids. Encourage them to pray also.

Scripture Memory Matthew 28:18-20

Scripture Memory Matthew 22:37-38   Have your children say this with you.

Jesus replied: "'Love the Lord your God with all your heart and with all your soul and with all your mind.' This is the first and greatest commandment. And the second is like it: 'Love your neighbor as yourself.' "

 While you read the Bible have your kids color the picture on their handwriting sheet.

 Bible Reading: Matthew 5-7, 22:34-40

Have the student(s) tell back what you read. Offer help along the way and kindly explain what you expect when they tell back a story. Be encouraging and compliment them.

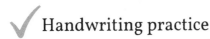 Handwriting practice

☼ Science

Do you remember last week how we learned that clouds are formed by water that has evaporated? Today we are going to learn about different kinds of clouds! There are 5 main types of clouds: cirrus, stratus, stratocumulus, cumulus, and cumulonimbus.

At creation, God separated the waters above from the waters below. A good explanation is that clouds are the waters above and the oceans, lakes, and rivers are the waters below. We are going to watch a video about clouds and do an experiment to show what happens when clouds get heavy and saturated with water.

▶ Watch "All About Clouds for Kids" from Free School on Youtube.

✓ Science Worksheet and Experiment

 SATURATED CLOUDS
SCIENCE ACTIVITY

We will need:

- A cotton ball
- Bowl of water
- A way to drip water (a medicine dropper works well)
- A cup

Directions:

- Hold your cotton ball over a cup.
- Slowly drip water onto the cotton ball being careful not to squeeze it.
- Once your cotton ball is fully saturated and can hold no more water, it will begin to flow out, symbolizing what happens when it rains. Clouds form and when they become heavy and saturated it rains!

*Extra: use cotton balls and glue to a sheet of construction paper to make models of the various kinds of clouds.

Practical Learning

- Each of the 50 states has a capital city. The capital of our state_____
- Washington D.C. is the capital of the United States
- There are 12 tribes of Israel
- Jesus had 12 disciples

Read to student:

Give time for them to answer questions and remind them when needed.

What do you remember most from hearing Jesus' sermon on the mount? Don't you think it would have been amazing to be there sitting on a mountain listening to Jesus?! I am so thankful that His Words were recorded for us to be able to read. I look forward to the day when I can sit and hear Him with all of our brothers and sisters in Christ!

 Language Arts Section in Student Workbook

 Observation Walk

Go on a walk outdoors and try to <u>observe</u> in creation what you <u>studied</u> in Science. Allow children to bring a notebook if they want to record their observations.
Use these three points to help start the discussion:

1	2	3
Look	**Factor**	**Observe**
Discuss what you are looking for. Find the location around your outdoor environment with the highest probability.	Talk about the possibilities of seeing what you studied. Is it cloudy? What kind of clouds do you see?	Did you find what you were looking for? Why? Why not? Did you learn something from seeing this in creation?

 CHECK LIST

- ☐ Worship
- ☐ Bible Reading
- ☐ Complete worksheets with each child

- ☐ Individual reading/reading out loud
- ☐ Math of choice

Let It Rain-
Michael W. Smith

Read to student:

The Scriptures we are going to read today remind us that clouds and rain come from God. Again and again this school year we will learn about the science behind particular parts of creation, but we must always come back to the knowledge of the truth that God is in control over all of it. If He says it doesn't happen, it doesn't happen. And if He says it does, it does. Our God is all-powerful. He defies "nature" again and again because He is the Creator. He can do whatever He pleases with what He made. He invites us to pray and seek Him and ask Him to intervene when we need Him to! The prayer of the righteous avails much. That means that things are truly accomplished when we pray. Real things happen. We don't just say words; the God of creation hears us!

 Please pray with your kids. Encourage them to pray also.

Scripture Memory Matthew 28:18-20

Scripture Memory Matthew 22:37-38   Have your children say this with you.

Jesus replied: "'Love the Lord your God with all your heart and with all your soul and with all your mind.' This is the first and greatest commandment. And the second is like it: 'Love your neighbor as yourself.' "

 While you read the Bible, have your children color the picture on their handwriting sheet. Older children may help with the reading.

 Bible Reading: 1 Kings 18:20-46, Psalm 147

Have the student(s) tell back what you read. Offer help along the way and kindly explain what you expect when they tell back a story. Be encouraging and compliment them.

 Handwriting Project   *Third and up write from memory.

At the end of each week, have your student practice their best handwriting. Remove this sheet and share with a friend, family member, or persecuted/imprisoned Christian (send through Voice of the Martyrs). Have children 3rd and up address the envelope and write their return address.

Practical Learning

Have students repeat these facts after you. *Give practical examples and hands on demonstrations when possible and when needed.

- Say the Lord's Prayer.
- Volume is another way we know how much of something there is, or how much is needed. We use these often in recipes. There are 8 ounces in one cup, 2 cups in a pint, 2 pints in a quart, and 4 quarts in a gallon.

Read to student:

Give time for them to answer questions and remind them when needed.

Let's review what we have learned this week.

Can you tell me something we learned from the Bible?

Do you remember what a continent is?

✓ Review anything from this week that your children struggled with. (Examples: sight words, letters)

✓ Language Arts Section in Student Workbook

📖 Read out loud to your children. This is a great time to read historical books. Be sure to choose books that are written from a Christian perspective or audit them closely for anything that isn't God-glorifying and true.

✓ Spend a few minutes with each child checking in on their reading progress. Make sure older children are able to decode words in syllables. Make sure younger children are recognizing their sight words within the text of a book.

CHECK LIST

- ☐ Worship
- ☐ Bible Reading
- ☐ Complete worksheets with each child
- ☐ Individual reading/reading out loud
- ☐ Math of choice

WEEK 4, DAY 1

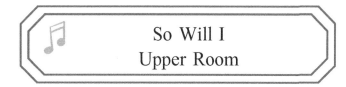
Read to student:

This is an exciting week! You get to choose a special project to do about the country that you chose to study. We will learn about the Israelites in the desert this week. There are lots of lessons to be learned from this! Do you know the story of the twelve spies? Do you remember which two spies believed God could give the people the Promised Land even though the enemies were large and intimidating? We want to have faith like Caleb and Joshua even if others don't! In the desert, God gave His people the rules He wanted them to live by and the instructions for how to worship Him, including the design of the Tabernacle. The plan was that the LORD would bring the people to the Promised Land and deliver it to them. However, because of their lack of faith, what should have been a rather short time in the desert turned into 40 years of living in the desert! God still loved and provided for His people, but He would not allow the unbelieving generation of the Israelites to enter the Promised Land. It is so important for us to believe God the first time He tells us something! We need to have faith in Him even when the circumstances look impossible.

 Please pray with your kids. Encourage them to pray also.

Scripture Memory Matthew 28:18-20

Scripture Memory Hebrew 11:1   Have your children say this with you.

"Now faith is confidence in what we hope for and assurance about what we do not see."

 While you read the Bible, have your kids color the picture on their handwriting sheet.

Bible Reading: Exodus 16, Numbers 13-14

Have the student(s) act out the story or a portion of the story that you read. Offer help with ideas and narration. You can make this as simple or complex as you wish.

 Handwriting practice

 Language Arts Section in Student Workbook

Review

- Tell me one of the 10 Commandments.
- What is Abraham called?
- Tell me one thing you have learned this year!
- Do you remember your memory verse from last week?
- Tell me one thing you are thankful for!

Read to student:

What did the Israelites eat in the desert? How did they get manna?
Isn't it sad that the people didn't believe in God even after all they have seen Him do? We have to be so careful that we don't see God's miracles and still fail to believe He can do more. We must live a life of consistent faith in the power of God that He can do what He says He can do. We have to trust Him for what seems impossible!
*Consider giving visuals of coriander and a lick of honey for the description of manna, The word manna is thought to mean "What is it?!"

 For our art time today, we are going to spend time working on our individual handicrafts. I will be available to help you if you need something. The Bible tells us to work the best we can in all we are doing. I want you to do your best work. It is good when we have skills that we are able to share with others. As we practice we get better at whatever we are working on! Don't get discouraged if you don't immediately catch on! You will get better the more you practice.

*Note to parents: Have your child work on skills that you chose for them at the beginning of the year. It is great to have them work on this more often than is built into our curriculum; however, every fourth week of our units will be a dedicated time to working on these.

 Read out loud to your children. This is a great time to read historical books. Be sure to choose books that are written from a Christian perspective or audit them closely for anything that isn't God glorifying and true. Children grades 1-5 should also spend time reading age-appropriate books.

CHECK LIST

- [ ] Worship
- [ ] Bible Reading
- [ ] Art Project

- [ ] Individual reading/reading out loud
- [ ] Complete worksheets with each child
- [ ] Math of choice

WEEK 4, DAY 2

Read to student:

The book of Deuteronomy is the end of Moses' life and the end of the Israelite's time wandering in the desert. It tells the story, a bit like a history book, of what had happened with the Israelites and most importantly, what they were to obey and do when they entered the Promised Land. It is essentially what Moses wanted to make ABSOLUTELY SURE the people knew before he died. He wanted them to remember to obey God because he knew it would be life for them. Although the desert was punishment, God was still with His people. He still blessed them and provided for them. He did not forget His promises to them!

*Note: As a parent, Deuteronomy is one of my favorite books because of the tremendous calls to action for parents. I am going to include references to a few verses I recommend reading. Remember that first and foremost the responsibility to teach our children falls to us, it is our responsibility before it is anyone else's responsibility. We cannot rely on our community, our friends, or our spiritual leaders to teach our kids. God commands us to teach and impress His ways upon them! Deuteronomy: 4:9-10, 29; 6:1-9; 8:17-20; 11:18-21.

 Please pray with your kids. Encourage them to pray also.

Scripture Memory Matthew 28:18-20

Scripture Memory Hebrew 11:1   Have your children say this with you.

"Now faith is confidence in what we hope for and assurance about what we do not see."

 While you read the Bible, have your kids color the picture on their handwriting sheet. *Extra long reading, provide a snack if desired.

 Bible Reading: Deuteronomy 1:22-2:7, 31:1-13, 34

Have the student(s) tell back what you read. Offer help along the way and kindly explain what you expect when they tell back a story. Be encouraging and compliment them.

 Handwriting practice

Practical Learning Have students repeat these facts after you.

- There are 5,280 feet in a mile.
- What did Jesus say the greatest commandments are? (Matt. 22:37-40)
  1. Love the LORD your God with all your heart, soul, and strength
  2. The second is like it, love your neighbor as yourself.
     All of the Law and prophets hang on these two commands.

✓ Language Arts Section in Student Workbook

 Read to student:

Today we get to do our first country project! Are you excited? Can you tell me why you chose the option you chose for our project? What is something that drew you to this country? Let's pray specifically for this country:

1. Pray for believers there to live for the Lord, love His Word, share the gospel, and seek first the kingdom of God.
2. Pray for their government officials to come to know Jesus and to have the wisdom to wisely lead their people. Pray for freedom to worship Jesus and for peace.
3. Pray for missionaries in this country and leaders of God's people. Pray for safety and that they would not grow weary in doing good.
4. Pray for the Lord to send more gospel workers into the harvest. Jesus said the harvest is plentiful but the laborers few! (Matthew 9:35-38)

Note: Encourage your child to do their best on their project. Help when needed. Don't forget to have them present their project to a family member or friend.

✓ Geography Section in Student Workbook

Read out loud to your children. This is a great time to read historical books. Be sure to choose books that are written from a Christian perspective or audit them closely for anything that isn't God glorifying and true. Children grades 1-5 should also spend time reading age-appropriate books.

CHECK LIST

- ☐ Worship
- ☐ Bible Reading
- ☐ Complete worksheets with each child
- ☐ Individual reading/reading out loud
- ☐ Math of choice

Cover the Sea-
Joshua Aaron

Read to student:

In John chapter five, Jesus talked to those who knew the Scriptures, yet did know Him. What do you think He meant? They "knew" Him as we think of knowing someone we speak with, yet they did know Him in a way that changed their life. Jesus is the source of eternal life, yet many of the people alive when Jesus was alive did not accept Him. Jesus said that if they believe Moses they would believe Him. Much of what we have read is written by Moses. Jesus said if we do not believe that, we will not believe in Him. Those are strong words! Many of the people He was speaking to appeared to believe, but they didn't really.

Listen carefully when we read today. I want to see if you can remember what day Jesus healed the man we will read about.

 Please pray with your kids. Encourage them to pray also.

Scripture Memory Matthew 28:18-20

Scripture Memory Hebrew 11:1   Have your children say this with you.

"Now faith is confidence in what we hope for and assurance about
what we do not see."

 While you read the Bible, have your kids color the picture on their handwriting sheet.

 Bible Reading: John 5

Have the student(s) tell back what you read. Offer help along the way and kindly explain what you expect when they tell back a story. Be encouraging and compliment them.

 Language Arts Section in Student Workbook

 # Science

Today we are going to learn about the waters below. In our reading today we read something very interesting about a pool of water. Do you remember what it was? Do you think this water was fresh water or salt water? How could healing occur in the water? God is so powerful. We can expect to see miracles when we walk with Him. When we think about the waters below, we can imagine oceans, rivers, streams, lakes, and ponds. Which of these is salt water? Which kind of water do we drink?

We have learned how important water is for the water cycle and how the earth is watered and able to produce food because of the water cycle (rain). Around each body of water, there is a special system called an ecosystem. It is really neat to learn about what plants, animals, fish, and reptiles can be found in and near specific bodies of water. Today, instead of our usual experiment we are going to do a special study of an ocean, river, or lake near where we live!

✓ Science Worksheet

 # WATER SYSTEM
SCIENCE ACTIVITY

Please help your child choose a river, lake, or ocean to study near your home to study. *If possible visit this location this week. If that is not possible, try to look at any pictures you may have and use the internet to help with your study.

- Choose one Bible verse to match your theme. (For example, Psalm 1:1-3 is about trees by a stream.)
- Help your child find pictures to copy or print to use for the plants and wildlife in this area.
- Discuss if this is important to your area. Does it provide food? Does it provide income? Do tourists visit this area? Are there businesses that are located on or near this?
- Help your child to understand how people are a God-ordained part of creation and that God created the world for us. We need to take care of what we have been given, but combat the idea that people are an issue for nature. People have souls, nature does not. People need saving by Jesus. Your child will likely encounter things like "Save the Earth," "Save the Bees," or other such campaigns. While managing resources is important, it is more important that our kids know and learn the Great Commission. People NEED to be saved by Jesus first and foremost. That is what is worth giving our lives to!

Practical Learning

- Say the books of the Bible either from memory or with song.
- For students that are confident readers, have them do a couple of Sword Drills. Sword Drills are fun competitions to see how fast you can find something in the Bible. Psalm 119:105, John 1:1, Romans 3:23

 Language Arts Section in Student Workbook

 Observation Walk

Go on a walk outdoors and try to observe in creation what you studied in science. Allow children to bring a notebook if they want to record their observations.
Use these three points to help start the discussion:

1

Look

Discuss what you are looking for. Find the location around your outdoor environment with the highest probability.

2

Factor

Talk about the possibilities of seeing what you studied. Can you visit the water system you studied?

3

Observe

Did you find what you were looking for? Why? Why not? Did you learn something from seeing this in creation?

CHECK LIST

- [ ] Worship
- [ ] Bible Reading
- [ ] Complete worksheets with each child
- [ ] Individual reading/reading out loud
- [ ] Math of choice

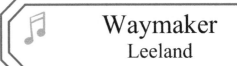

Waymaker
Leeland

Read to student:

God's Word is full of so much wisdom and comfort. We can learn so many things from what God created, and the Bible gives some great examples. Today we are going to read about what we can learn from an ant. Can you guess what that might be?

God loves us so much! He forgives us for our sins and He desires to know us. Do you know what compassion is? Compassion is showing sympathy and desiring to relieve someone's distress. The Bible tells us that God is compassionate. When Jesus walked the earth He had the compassion as God to heal people and deliver them! We can pray that God will give us compassion for others. True compassion desires to show the world that Jesus is the best answer to suffering and distress.

 Please pray with your kids. Encourage them to pray also.

Scripture Memory Matthew 28:18-20

Scripture Memory Hebrew 11:1   Have your children say this with you.

"Now faith is confidence in what we hope for and assurance about what we do not see."

 While you read the Bible, have your children color the picture on their handwriting sheet. Older children may help with the reading.

 Bible Reading: Psalm 103, Proverbs 6

Have the student(s) tell back what you read. Offer help along the way and kindly explain what you expect when they tell back a story. Be encouraging and compliment them.

 Handwriting Project   *Third and up write from memory.

At the end of each week, have your student practice their best handwriting. Remove this sheet and share with a friend, family member, or persecuted/imprisoned Christian (send through Voice of the Martyrs). Have children 3rd and up address the envelope and write their return address.

End of unit review:

Give time for them to answer questions and remind them when needed.

We are finished with our second unit of school! Wow! Great job. I am enjoying teaching you and learning with you. Let's do a review of some of the things we have learned!

Can you tell me something we learned from the Bible?

Is there one verse or lesson that really helped you?
Did the LORD comfort or convict you in any area?

What is something you learned about water?

Tell me a historical person you most enjoyed learning about. Why did you enjoy their story?

What was your favorite thing you learned about Africa?

✓ Review anything from this week that your children struggled with. (Examples: sight words, letters)

✓ Language Arts Section in Student Workbook

📖 Read out loud to your children. This is a great time to read historical books. Be sure to choose books that are written from a Christian perspective or audit them closely for anything that isn't God-glorifying and true.

✓ Spend a few minutes with each child checking in on their reading progress. Make sure older children are able to decode words into syllables. Make sure younger children are recognizing their sight words within the text of a book.

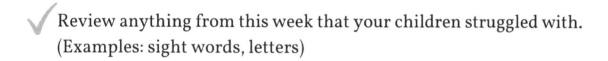

CHECK LIST

- [ ] Worship
- [ ] Bible Reading
- [ ] Complete worksheets with each child
- [ ] Individual reading/reading out loud
- [ ] Math of choice

Mini-Unit Study Plan

✓ Choose a topic

✓ Find needed resources- videos, websites, books

✓ Choose activities: field trip, experiment, movie

✓ Find Scriptures that many apply

① Plan

Work with your child(ren) to come up with the best study for your family. Make a plan and allow them to be involved in finding resources and ideas.

② Learn

Choose ways that learning will be involved. Examples include a write up, making lists, books to read, and more

③ Enjoy

Have fun! Allow your child to talk to others about their experience. Try to enjoy this week together and foster a desire to learn more.

WEEK 5 DAILY CHECK LIST

☐ Unit Study ☐ Math of choice

☐ Unit Study ☐ Math of choice

☐ Unit Study ☐ Math of choice

☐ Unit Study ☐ Math of choice

UNIT
three

GOSPEL FOCUS & EYES ON JESUS

It's easy part way through the school year to lose focus of our "why" and the purpose of educating our children with a strong Biblical foundation. Let's pause and take time to remember our why and have eternity in our hearts as we journey through homeschooling. In each of the remaining units, there will be a small section for you, as the parent, to re-focus your heart on the Lord. Take time to make sure your children know Jesus personally and that through their education they are learning to love the Lord with all their heart, soul, strength, and mind. Think of tangible ways to love your neighbor as yourself.

PRAY

Pause and intentionally pray over your school time. Ask the Lord to work through the time you spend educating your children to give you and your children a kingdom-first perspective. Ask the Lord to help you keep your eyes on Jesus. Seek the Lord for opportunities and ways you and your children can share the gospel and pray for anyone you have shared the gospel with. Pray for each of your children that they would know and serve the Lord.

QUESTIONS

1. Am I being intentional with our homeschool time?
2. Are we simply checking boxes or are my children learning to love Jesus and others through our schooling?
3. Do I feel burned out? If so, seek the Lord for new strength
4. How can I best use the time I have with my children? Are we too busy to focus on what matters most?
5. Have I let distractions creep into our day that we need to reduce?

EXTRA
Resources

UNIT VERSE

Say this verse when prompted with your kids. The goal with this verse is not perfect memorization in younger grades. The goal is Scripture truth being on their heart and mind.

*Aim for weekly memory verses to be quoted by each child and written from memory for grades 4-5.

"This, then, is how you should pray: '"Our Father in heaven, hallowed be your name, your kingdom come, your will be done, on earth as it is in heaven. Give us today our daily bread. And forgive us our debts, as we also have forgiven our debtors. And lead us not into temptation, but deliver us from the evil one.'" Matthew 6:9-13

PRAYER REQUESTS

Record things you and your children would like to pray over here. Be sure to check back and praise the Lord when He answers. Prompt your kids to think about praying for others. Read Matthew 6:9-13 for how Jesus taught us to pray. As you study the Word, notice the pattern of Biblical prayers and prayer requests and try to learn from the Word.

_____	_____
_____	_____
_____	_____
_____	_____

 WEEK 1, DAY 1

 I Am Not Alone- Kari Jobe

Read to student:

Welcome to our next unit! In unit three we will be studying Asia, dry land, and more of the Bible. We are going to start by learning about how the Israelites got to the Promised Land. Do you remember whom God called to lead His people after Moses? That's right, Joshua! After 40 years in the desert, God's people were finally able to enter the Promised Land. Have you ever been nervous about something? Maybe a big job that you didn't feel prepared for? Perhaps that is how Joshua felt! Again and again, Moses, God, and others reminded Joshua to be strong and courageous. They reminded him that God would be with him. A good deal of the book of Joshua is about the military victories that God gave His people as they entered the Promised Land to claim it as their inheritance. Do you remember Abraham? God promised Abraham, Isaac, and Jacob this land! He promised that their descendants would be numerous and that He would bring them into the land that He had promised. God is faithful and He always keeps His promises. If God says something, we can always believe Him. There is a lot of this story that we aren't going to read right now but if you are interested in reading more about how the Israelites conquered the land with God's help, you can read the rest of the book of Joshua for individual reading. For now, let's get started!

 Please pray with your kids. Encourage them to pray also.

Scripture Memory Matthew 6:9-13

Scripture Memory Joshua 1:9   Have your children say this with you.

"Have I not commanded you? Be strong and courageous. Do not be afraid; do not be discouraged, for the Lord your God will be with you wherever you go."

 While you read the Bible, have your kids color their sheet in their workbook.

 Bible Reading: Joshua 1-3

Have the student(s) tell back what you read. Offer help along the way and kindly explain what you expect when they tell back a story. Be encouraging and compliment.

 Handwriting practice

Review

- Say the ABCs
- (1st +) Do you remember what nouns and verbs are? (Noun- person, place, or thing. Verb- a word that shows action.)
- (1st +) When do we capitalize the first letter of a word? (Beginning of a sentence, proper noun, and the word I.)
- We are going to learn (practice) the calendar. Do you know many days are in a week? How many months are in a year?
  Say the days of the week and the months of the year.

 Language Arts Section in Student Workbook

Read to student:

Do you remember the name of the lady who helped the spies to hide? How did she hide them? What did she have to hang out her window so that she and her family would be saved?
God is kind and compassionate. Throughout Scripture, we see that God had mercy on people who helped His people. He received those who were considered foreigners.

 This week for our art project we are going to learn a skill that is both practical and useful, knot tying, There are many different styles of knots. Some are used for securing objects, some for fishing, some for safety, and some are decorative. Choose a category to focus on and find online videos and sources to practice. *Optional: Use a scarlet cord to incorporate our Bible lesson about Rahab if you wish. Discuss that she likely would have needed a way to secure the scarlet cord in her window.

 Read out loud to your children, this is a great time to read historical books. Be sure to choose books that are written from a Christian perspective or audit them closely for anything that isn't God-glorifying and true. Children grades 1-5 should also spend time reading age-appropriate books.

CHECK LIST

- ☐ Worship
- ☐ Bible Reading
- ☐ Art Project

- ☐ Individual reading/reading out loud
- ☐ Complete worksheets with each child
- ☐ Math of choice

WEEK 1, DAY 2

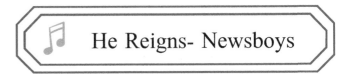

He Reigns- Newsboys

Read to student:

Do you remember when you were very small? A baby, perhaps just a small child? I want you to imagine something with me for a moment. Pretend you were an Israelite child who left Egypt as a small child. Before you could remember anything. Imagine you had lived your entire life in the desert. What would you have been eating? Yep, mostly manna. That's right! Imagine living your entire life having your parents tell you that you would enter the Promised Land. You would have been looking forward to this very significant event for many, many years! Nearly your entire life! How would you feel if it was the day to set foot in the land God had promised? Can you imagine the main food you had relied on stopped falling from heaven? Maybe you would be excited, maybe a little nervous. Think about this as I read from the Bible to you today. Use your imagination and consider how the people must have felt!

 Please pray with your kids. Encourage them to pray also.

Scripture Memory Matthew 6:9-13

Scripture Memory Joshua 1:9   Have your children say this with you.

"Have I not commanded you? Be strong and courageous. Do not be afraid; do not be discouraged, for the Lord your God will be with you wherever you go."

 While you read the Bible have your kids color their sheet in their workbook.

 Bible Reading: Joshua 4-6, 14:6-15

Have the student(s) tell back what you read. Offer help along the way and kindly explain what you expect when they tell back a story. Be encouraging and compliment them.

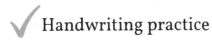 Handwriting practice

Practical Learning Have students repeat these facts after you.

- There are 24 hours in a day, 60 minutes in an hour, and 60 seconds in a minute.
- There are 52 weeks in a year and 7 days in a week.
- "Thirty days hath September, April, June, and November; all the rest have 31 except February which has 28, except in a leap year when it has 29."
- There are 365 days in a year, and a leap year has 366.

 Language Arts Section in Student Workbook

 Look at a globe or map with your child and show them Asia. Point out different countries in Asia, and ask them to begin thinking about which country they would like to study more.

Read to student:

Today we are going to begin learning about Asia! Asia is mentioned in the Bible several times, primarily in the NT. Asia is both the largest continent and the most populated. There are 48 countries in Asia and more than 4 billion people live there! Wow! A significant number of our brothers and sisters in Christ live in Asia. In some places, it is very challenging to be a Christian. In some places, it is illegal. But God's Word always continues to spread and flourish!

Read a continent book about Asia.

 Continent Study in Student Workbook

Read out loud to your children. This is a great time to read historical books. Be sure to choose books that are written from a Christian perspective or audit them closely for anything that isn't God-glorifying and true. Children grades 1-5 should also spend time reading age-appropriate books.

CHECK LIST

- [ ] Worship
- [ ] Bible Reading
- [ ] Complete worksheets with each child
- [ ] Individual reading/reading out loud
- [ ] Math of choice

WEEK 1, DAY 3

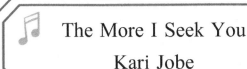

♫ The More I Seek You

Kari Jobe

Read to student:

Yesterday we learned that when the people entered the Promised Land, the manna stopped. Do you think God could still miraculously provide food for people in other ways? Do you know any Bible stories about this?

Today we are going to read about an awesome miracle that Jesus did! Listen for what Jesus said about manna. The people who ate the manna that God provided were the ancestors of the people Jesus was speaking to. An ancestor is your great, great, great, great (and even more greats!) grandparents. They are people in your family who lived long before you.

Some of the things that Jesus said were hard for people to understand. Some of these things are still hard for us to understand, but we can trust Jesus that what He said is always true and right.

The Bible: the inspired Word of God ▶ Learn the books of the Bible to song

66 books make up one, big book

39 books in the OT, 27 books in the NT

 Please pray with your kids. Encourage them to pray also.

Scripture Memory Matthew 6:9-13

Scripture Memory Joshua 1:9   Have your children say this with you.

"Have I not commanded you? Be strong and courageous. Do not be afraid; do not be discouraged, for the Lord your God will be with you wherever you go."

 While you read the Bible, have your kids color their sheet in their workbook.

📖 Bible Reading: John 5

Have the student(s) tell back what you read. Offer help along the way and kindly explain what you expect when they tell back a story. Be encouraging and compliment them.

 Handwriting practice

 # Science

On the third day of creation, God spoke dry land into existence and called vegetation to spring up. Vegetation is plants and trees. God is very specific in talking about seed-bearing plants and trees. I want you to listen very closely for a minute and see what you hear God say about seed-bearing plants and trees. READ Genesis 1:9-13. Each plant bore seeds according to its kind. Seeds give plants the ability to reproduce and grow more, new plants. Later God says these are good for food! Seeds are how we grow gardens, how food is produced, and how the earth is filled with beautiful plants. Vegetation is essential for life. Without plants, we wouldn't have food or clean air.

 # ACCORDING TO THEIR KIND
SCIENCE ACTIVITY

We will need:
- 3 kinds of fruit with seeds (examples: apples, pears, grapes with seeds, dates, peppers, kiwi, tomatoes, oranges with seeds, lemons)
- The ability to cut the fruit open

We are going to do a fun experiment! This experiment involves making a snack! We are going to choose 3 different kinds of fruit with seeds. You are going to draw a picture of each seed and what kind of fruit it comes from. Do you notice the difference in kinds?

Discuss with your child if the fruit had one seed or many seeds.

Use the fruit to come up with a fun design to make for a snack plate.

▶ Watch "Facts About Seeds" from The Ranger Zak Show on Youtube.

 Science Worksheet

Practical Learning
Present these for your family and without causing your kids to feel afraid. They are wise things we must teach.

- What do we do in the event of a fire? *Also teach stop, drop, and roll
- What do we do in the event of a natural disaster *fill in with applicable events such as earthquakes, tornadoes, or other.
- Should you ever go with a stranger? NO! Even if they tell you that they know your mom and dad you need to run and immediately go find one of your parents.

 Language Arts Section in Student Workbook

 Observation Walk

Go on a walk outdoors and try to <u>observe</u> in creation what you <u>studied</u> in Science. Allow children to bring a notebook if they want to record their observations.
Use these three points to help start the discussion:

1	2	3
## Look	## Factor	## Observe
Discuss what you are looking for. Find the location around your outdoor environment with the highest probability.	Talk about the possibilities of seeing what you studied. Is it currently the season you can see seeds?	Did you find what you were looking for? Why? Why not? Did you learn something from seeing this in creation?

 CHECK LIST

☐ Worship

☐ Bible Reading

☐ Complete worksheets with each child

 ☐ Individual reading/reading out loud

 ☐ Math of choice

WEEK 1, DAY 4

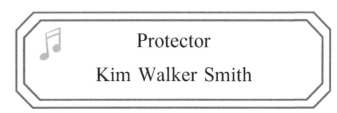

Protector

Kim Walker Smith

Read to student:

Let's play Bible trivia today! I am going to ask questions, you tell me the right answer as fast as you can. (In our family we offer chocolate chips or other small treats for correct answers. It makes Bible trivia extra sweet and the kids really enjoy it. If you are interested in more questions than are provided, download our free Bible trivia printable on www.lampandlightmerchandise.com.)

Bible Trivia

1. How many days did it take God to create the heavens and the earth?
2. How many disciples did Jesus have?
3. What river did God part for the Israelites?
4. How many days did it take for the walls of Jericho to fall?
5. Whom did God send to deliver His people from slavery in Egypt?
6. How many loaves and fish did Jesus use to multiply to feed the people?
7. What was Jesus' first public miracle?
8. How can we be saved?

 Please pray with your kids. Encourage them to pray also.

Scripture Memory Matthew 6:9-13

Scripture Memory Joshua 1:9   Have your children say this with you.

"Have I not commanded you? Be strong and courageous. Do not be afraid; do not be discouraged, for the Lord your God will be with you wherever you go."

 While you read the Bibl,e have your children color the picture on their handwriting sheet. Older children may help with the reading.

 Bible Reading: Psalm 16, Proverbs 11

Have the student(s) tell back what you read. Offer help along the way and kindly explain what you expect when they tell back a story. Be encouraging and compliment them.

✓ Handwriting Project   *Third and up write from memory.

At the end of each week have your student practice their best handwriting. Remove this sheet and share with a friend, family member, or persecuted/imprisoned Christian (send through Voice of the Martyrs). Have children 3rd and up address the envelope and write their return address.

Practical Learning

Have students repeat these facts after you. *Give practical examples and hands on demonstrations when possible and when needed.

- Say the Armor of God (Helmet of salvation, the breastplate of righteousness, the belt of truth, feet shod with the readiness of the gospel of peace, shield of faith, sword of the Spirit which is the Word of God.
- Measurement is broken down into units. An inch is a common unit of measurement. There are 12 inches in a foot, and 3 feet in a yard.

✓ Review anything from this week that your children struggled with. (Examples: Sight words, letters)

✓ Language Arts Section in Student Workbook

📖 Read out loud to your children. This is a great time to read historical books. Be sure to choose books that are written from a Christian perspective or audit them closely for anything that isn't God-glorifying and true. Children grades 1-5 should also spend time reading age-appropriate books.

CHECK LIST

- ☐ Worship
- ☐ Bible Reading
- ☐ Complete worksheets with each child
- ☐ Individual reading/reading out loud
- ☐ Math of choice

 WEEK 2, DAY 1

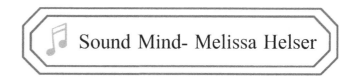 ♪ Sound Mind- Melissa Helser

Read to student:

Today we are going to watch a Bible video about the book of Judges. It is an interesting and sometimes challenging book of the Bible.

*NOTE to parents: We only spend one day on the book of Judges. Use your discretion as a parent to decide if you wish to read more to your children now or wait until they are older.

▶ Watch "Overview: Judges" from The Bible Project on YouTube

 Please pray with your kids. Encourage them to pray also.

Scripture Memory Matthew 6:9-13

Scripture Memory 1 Samuel 15:22   Have your children say this with you.

"But Samuel replied: 'Does the Lord delight in burnt offerings and sacrifice as much as in obeying the Lord? To obey is better than sacrifice, and to heed is better than the fat of rams.'"

✓ While you read the Bible, have your kids color the picture on their handwriting sheet.

📖 Bible Reading: Judges 2

Spend a few minutes discussing what happens when people don't follow God. Try to ask your children thought-provoking questions about the difference between obeying rules that are for our good and disobeying.

Handwriting practice

Language Arts Section in Student Workbook

Review + Focus

- What continent did we study in our last unit? Tell me one fact about it!
- How would you share the gospel with someone? Start with telling them who Jesus is. (Help as needed, encourage your kids to use what they practice to really share about Jesus with kids they encounter in your neighborhood, at the park, or otherwise.)
- Tell me one prayer that God has answered for you!
- Tell me one thing you are thankful for!

 Art Project: Herb Planter
- Tin can (poke holes in the bottom)
- Fabric or paint
- Hot glue or Modge Podge
-Cover the can in fabric or paint to make a pretty planter (see Lampandlight on Pinterest for ideas). Save this planter because we will use it to plant a seed later this week!

Read out loud to your children. This is a great time to read historical books. Be sure to choose books that are written from a Christian perspective or audit them closely for anything that isn't God-glorifying and true. Children grades 1-5 should also spend time reading age-appropriate books.

CHECK LIST

☐ Worship

☐ Bible Reading

☐ Art Project

☐ Individual reading/reading out loud

☐ Complete worksheets with each child

☐ Math of choice

WEEK 2, DAY 2

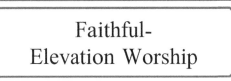

♪ Faithful-
Elevation Worship

Read to student:

Have you heard of Ruth or Naomi before? Today we are going to learn about their story from the Bible. It is a beautiful and redemptive story.   Ruth is especially neat because she was not an Israelite by birth, but she chose to go with her mother-in-law to serve the one, true God, Yahweh. What makes Ruth even more special is that she is in the lineage of Jesus! As we read this story, imagine what it would be like to leave your family and country. Would that be worth it? Do you think it was hard for Ruth? God certainly blessed her for her willingness!

 Please pray with your kids. Encourage them to pray also.

Scripture Memory Matthew 6:9-13

Scripture Memory 1 Samuel 15:22   Have your children say this with you.

"But Samuel replied: 'Does the Lord delight in burnt offerings and sacrifice as much as in obeying the Lord? To obey is better than sacrifice, and to heed is better than the fat of rams.'"

 While you read the Bible, have your kids color the picture on their handwriting sheet.

 Bible Reading: The Book of Ruth

*This reading is long; you may wish to provide a snack.
Have the student(s) tell back what you read. Offer help along the way and kindly explain what you expect when they tell back a story. Be encouraging and compliment them.

 Handwriting practice

Practical Learning Have students repeat these facts after you.

- A penny is worth 1 cent, a nickel is worth 5 cents, a dime is worth 10 cents, and a quarter is worth 25 cents.
- There are 100 cents in a dollar.
- For older kids, challenge them to tell you what amount of money different combinations of coins make.

 Language Arts Section in Student Workbook

 Read to student:

Do you remember what you learned last week about Asia? Today we are going to have some fun with what we learned! We are going to make the information you learned into a visual report that you can share with others. There is a sheet in your workbook to help you get started.

Things to consider encouraging your child to add:
- Visual appeal with colors, themes, and facts
- Stickers, printed or magazine images, or drawings
- Number of countries
- Top natural resources
- Main religion, percent of known Christians *Be sure to share that this isn't always accurate if a country has laws against Christianity. We could have brothers and sisters in Christ not openly declaring their religion.
- Main bodies of water
- Any significant landmarks, both natural and man-made

Read out loud to your children. This is a great time to read historical books. Be sure to choose books that are written from a Christian perspective or audit them closely for anything that isn't God-glorifying and true. Children grades 1-5 should also spend time reading age-appropriate books.

CHECK LIST

- ☐ Worship
- ☐ Bible Reading
- ☐ Complete worksheets with each child
- ☐ Individual reading/reading out loud
- ☐ Math of choice

WEEK 2, DAY 3

High and Lifted Up-
Sean Feucht

Read to student:

Today we start a journey into the next significant portion of Israel's history. We will meet Samuel, who is the man God called from before his birth as a prophet to His people. Samuel anointed the first two kings of Israel, which is the next portion of the Bible we will begin studying next week.

Did you enjoy the Bible Project video we watched about Judges? We are going to watch a similar video about 1 Samuel!

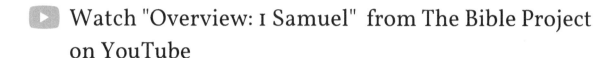

▶ Watch "Overview: 1 Samuel" from The Bible Project on YouTube

 Please pray with your kids. Encourage them to pray also.

Scripture Memory Matthew 6:9-13

Scripture Memory 1 Samuel 15:22   Have your children say this with you.

"But Samuel replied: 'Does the Lord delight in burnt offerings and sacrifice as much as in obeying the Lord? To obey is better than sacrifice, and to heed is better than the fat of rams.'"

✓ While you read the Bible, have your kids color the picture on their handwriting sheet.

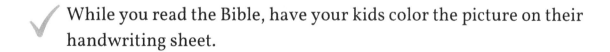 Bible Reading: 1 Samuel 1-2:11,3

Have the student(s) tell back what you read. Offer help along the way and kindly explain what you expect when they tell back a story. Be encouraging and compliment them.

✓ Handwriting practice

 # Science

Did you know that plants have different phases in their life? Remember the seeds that we learned about last week? Each little seed can produce a whole new plant! Given the right conditions, a seed will germinate, sprout, produce a seedling, and eventually grow into a mature plant. Mature plants flower and produce new seeds to start the cycle over. When the same process happens again and again we call it a cycle. Today we are going to work on learning about the life cycle of a plant.

▶ ## Watch "How Does a Seed Become a Plant?" from SciShowKids on Youtube.

✓ ### Science Worksheet and Experiment

 ## SOW & GROW
SCIENCE ACTIVITY

Grab your planter we made earlier this week and let's sow a seed!

We will need:
- Planter
- Soil
- Seed- herbs are a great choice
- Water

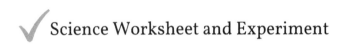

- Fill your planter with soil
- Read the instructions on your seed packet and plant your seeds accordingly
- Water your seeds
- Place in a sunny window
- Continue to water over the next several weeks. Watch and record how long it takes for your seeds to sprout (germinate) and grow.

Practical Learning Present these for your family and without causing your kids to feel afraid. They are wise things we must teach.

- What do we do in the event of a fire? *Also teach stop, drop, and roll
- What do we do in the event of a natural disaster *fill in with applicable events such as earthquakes, tornadoes, or other.
- Should you ever go with a stranger? NO! Even if they tell you that they know your mom and dad, you need to run and immediately go find one of your parents.

 Language Arts Section in Student Workbook

 Observation Walk

Go on a walk outdoors and try to <u>observe</u> in creation what you <u>studied</u> in Science. Allow children to bring a notebook if they want to record their observations.
Use these three points to help start the discussion:

Look

Discuss what you are looking for. Find the location around your outdoor environment with the highest probability.

Factor

Talk about the possibilities of seeing what you studied. Is it warm enough for plants to grow? What phases of plant life can you find?

Observe

Did you find what you were looking for? Why? Why not? Did you learn something from seeing this in creation?

CHECK LIST

- ☐ Worship
- ☐ Bible Reading
- ☐ Complete worksheets with each child
- ☐ Individual reading/reading out loud
- ☐ Math of choice

WEEK 2, DAY 4

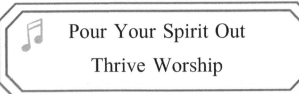

Pour Your Spirit Out
Thrive Worship

Read to student:

We are going to backtrack in Jesus' story today so you can hear the song that Mary, Jesus' mother sang. Pay careful attention because some parts of her song sound similar to what Hannah sang when she was blessed with Samuel.

As we read about Jesus' birth, imagine each of the people who are mentioned in this story and how the coming of the Messiah impacted their life.

Can you imagine what it would be like to see an angel?! Would you be startled? Do you think you would believe the message like Mary or question like Zechariah? How were Mary and Zechariah's questions different?

 Please pray with your kids. Encourage them to pray also.

Scripture Memory Matthew 6:9-13

Scripture Memory 1 Samuel 15:22   Have your children say this with you.

"But Samuel replied: "Does the Lord delight in burnt offerings and sacrifice as much as in obeying the Lord? To obey is better than sacrifice, and to heed is better than the fat of rams."

✓ While you read the Bible, have your children color the picture on their handwriting sheet. Older children may help with the reading.

📖 Bible Reading: Luke 1-2

Have the student(s) tell back what you read. Offer help along the way and kindly explain what you expect when they tell back a story. Be encouraging and compliment them.

✓ Handwriting Project   *Third and up write from memory.

At the end of each week, have your student practice their best handwriting. Remove this sheet and share with a friend, family member, or persecuted/imprisoned Christian (send through Voice of the Martyrs). Have children 3rd and up address the envelope and write their return address.

Practical Learning

Have students repeat these facts after you. *Give practical examples and hands-on demonstrations when possible and when needed.

- Say the fruits of the Spirit: love, joy, peace, patience, kindness, goodness, faithfulness, gentleness, and self-control.
- Weight is how we know how heavy something is. An ounce is a small unit of weight. There are 16 ounces in a pound.

Read to student:

Give time for them to answer questions and remind them when needed.

Let's review what we have learned this week.

Can you tell me something we learned from the Bible?

Tell me one fact about Asia.

✓ Review anything from this week that your children struggled with. (Examples: sight words, letters)

✓ Language Arts Section in Student Workbook

📖 Read out loud to your children. This is a great time to read historical books. Be sure to choose books that are written from a Christian perspective or audit them closely for anything that isn't God-glorifying and true. Children grades 1-5 should also spend time reading age-appropriate books.

✓ Help your child with their worksheet and report about a historical figure.

If you have not completed a book about a historical figure, do your best to help your child find a historical person of interest to use for this exercise. Add words your child may struggle with when writing to next week's spelling list.

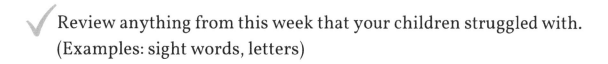

CHECK LIST

- ☐ Worship
- ☐ Bible Reading
- ☐ Complete worksheets with each child
- ☐ Individual reading/reading out loud
- ☐ Math of choice

WEEK 3, DAY 1

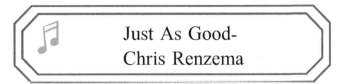

♪ Just As Good-
Chris Renzema

Read to student:

God's people wanted a king like the nations around them. Kings rule and have authority in a land. God wanted to be the only King of His people, but they insisted on having a human king. Today we are going to read about Israel, Samuel, and God's conversation about this issue. Do you know who the top ruler in our country is? In the USA, the President is the correct answer. (Note: You may also wish to mention the balance of power and how a president is different from a king. Examples of the ways they are different: presidents are elected by the people of their country through voting, the presidency is not passed down within a family, and the president must work within the balance of power.)

 Please pray with your kids. Encourage them to pray also.

Scripture Memory Matthew 6:9-13

Scripture Memory I Samuel 12:24   Have your children say this with you.

"But be sure to fear the Lord and serve him faithfully with all your heart; consider what great things he has done for you."

✓ While you read the Bible, have your kids color the picture on their handwriting sheet.

 Bible Reading: I Samuel 7-10

Have the student(s) act out the story or a portion of the story that you read. Offer help with ideas and narration. You can make this as simple or complex as you wish.

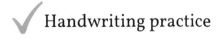 Handwriting practice

✓ Language Arts Section in Student Workbook

Review

- How many days did it take God to create the world?
- Who was the first king of Israel?
- Who anointed him to be king?
- Tell me the continents we have studied so far.
- Do you remember your memory verse from last week?
- How did God save Moses?
- Tell me one thing you are thankful for!

 Earlier this year in our list of supplies from creation, you were prompted to dry flowers for this project. If you didn't that is ok, simply have your child draw or paint a flower. We are going to make bookmarks! If you are able to laminate or tape these, please do so as they will last longer.

You will need:
- Pretty paper
- A flower
- Tape or laminator sheet
- Hole punch
- Ribbon

Please visit lampandlightliving on Pinterest and view the board "Unit 3" for ideas.

Read out loud to your children. This is a great time to read historical books. Be sure to choose books that are written from a Christian perspective or audit them closely for anything that isn't God-glorifying and true. Children grades 1-5 should also spend time reading age-appropriate books.

CHECK LIST

☐ Worship

☐ Bible Reading

☐ Art Project

☐ Individual reading/reading out loud

☐ Complete worksheets with each child

☐ Math of choice

WEEK 3, DAY 2

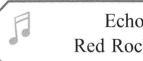

Echo Holy-
Red Rocks Worship

Read to student:

Yesterday we learned about Israel's first king. Sadly, King Saul did not follow God wholeheartedly. This led God to reject Saul as the king of Israel. God chose David to be the king of Israel instead of Saul. Throughout David's life, he greatly pleased the LORD. He trusted God, repented when he sinned, and humbly sought the LORD. Because he was a man after God's own heart, God promised him that he would always have a descendant on the throne. Jesus is a descendant of David, so David does indeed have a descendant on the throne!

 Please pray with your kids. Encourage them to pray also.

Scripture Memory Matthew 6:9-13

Scripture Memory 1 Samuel 12:24   Have your children say this with you.

"But be sure to fear the Lord and serve him faithfully with all your heart; consider what great things he has done for you."

 While you read the Bible, have your kids color the picture on their handwriting sheet.

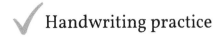 Bible Reading: 1 Samuel 15-18:16

Have the student(s) tell back what you read. Offer help along the way and kindly explain what you expect when they tell back a story. Be encouraging and compliment them.

✓ Handwriting practice

Practical Learning   Have students repeat these facts after you.

- Freezing temperature of water is 32 degrees F.
- Boiling temperature of water is 212 degrees F.
- Water expands when it freezes.
- Water can be in different forms. It can be a liquid, a solid (ice), and a gas (steam).

 Language Arts Section in Student Workbook

 Read to student:

Today we are going to study one country from the continent of Asia. If you have not already done so, please choose a country on the continent of Asia to study. We are going to work together to find the answers to the questions on your worksheet. Next week we will choose a project to do for the country you chose. You will have different options to choose from. You may look ahead in your book now and decide which project you will do. While we study, we will look for information to prepare for next week.

Every country is unique. They have distinct features both geographically and culturally. Some countries are very diverse. The United States gives us a good example. There are different areas of the United States that have very different cultures. How we talk even sounds a little bit different! The styles of food in different parts of the country vary, the climate varies, and the natural resources and job opportunities vary. While there is variation within a country, a country shares a common government, currency (money), main language, and laws.

 Read out loud to your children. This is a great time to read historical books. Be sure to choose books that are written from a Christian perspective or audit them closely for anything that isn't God-glorifying and true. Children grades 1-5 should also spend time reading age-appropriate books.

CHECK LIST

- [ ] Worship
- [ ] Bible Reading
- [ ] Complete worksheets with each child
- [ ] Individual reading/reading out loud
- [ ] Math of choice

WEEK 3, DAY 3

 Throne Room
Kim Walker-Smith

Read to student:

Do you know anyone who behaves well all of the time?

We can never be good on our own, but praise God through Jesus we have forgiveness for our sins! The only human who ever lived without sinning is Jesus. As we remember Israel's kings, we sometimes categorize them as "bad" or "good." Essentially "good" only means that they chose to serve God. Many of the kings that we consider good still made huge mistakes. As we learn about the kings of Israel, there is a deep longing that perhaps one of them will be fully righteous! And finally, there was. Jesus! A baby born into humanity, not royalty. A humble healer instead of a reigning king. Jesus is exactly whom we long for as we read of the many failures of Israel, yet when He came many did not realize He was the King of kings. Jesus is on His throne reigning in heaven now, waiting for His enemies to be made His footstool. When He came to earth, it was not with a crown or a throne. He came to sacrifice his all for us. Today we will read two Psalms that point to Jesus written many, many years before He was born.

 Please pray with your kids. Encourage them to pray also.

Scripture Memory Matthew 6:9-13

Scripture Memory I Samuel 12:24   Have your children say this with you.

"But be sure to fear the Lord and serve him faithfully with all your heart; consider what great things he has done for you."

 While you read the Bible, have your kids color the picture on their handwriting sheet.

 Bible Reading: Psalm 2, 110

Have the student(s) tell back what you read. Offer help along the way and kindly explain what you expect when they tell back a story. Be encouraging and compliment them.

 Handwriting practice

🔅 Science

Last week we learned about the life cycle of plants. How are the seeds that you planted doing? Have they sprouted yet?

Today we are going to look at the parts of a fully grown plant! Can you tell me any parts of a plant?

Let's play a game! We are going to name as many different varieties of plants as we can in two minutes. I'll write them down and we will see how many we can get! Let's go!

 *Set a timer for 2 minutes and play this game with your student.

▶ Watch "Parts of Plant for Kids" from Learn Bright on Youtube.

✓ Science Worksheet and Experiment

EDIBLE PLANTS
SCIENCE ACTIVITY

You will need:

- Root vegetable- potato, carrot, beet, etc.
- Leafy veggies- lettuce, spinach, collards, or any other edible greens
- A "fruit" veggie- tomato, pepper, eggplant, cucumber
- A seed- sunflower, pumpkin, bean
- Creativity or a recipe!

Directions:

Lay each ingredient out and discuss which part of the plant it represents.

Talk about the many ways we use the different parts of the plant and the different stages of growth. Brainstorm together and come up with a meal that you can make using the ingredients from each different part of the plants that you have chosen. Discuss different parts of the plant that are edible (example: carrot tops are edible and make a great pesto). Talk about any parts of the plant that may not be edible. Discuss what climate these ingredients grow in and if they grow where you live. If they do not grow where you live, or the season is wrong, use this as an opportunity to talk about how food gets to the grocery store, where it comes from, who grows it, and how fresh it is (or isn't).

Practical Learning

- Each of the 50 states has a capital city. The capital of our state_____
- Washington D.C. is the capital of the United States
- There are 12 tribes of Israel
- Jesus had 12 disciples

 Language Arts Section in Student Workbook

 Observation Walk

Go on a walk outdoors and try to <u>observe</u> in creation what you <u>studied</u> in Science. Allow children to bring a notebook if they want to record their observations.
Use these three points to help start the discussion:

1

Look

Discuss what you are looking for. Find the location around your outdoor environment with the highest probability.

2

Factor

Talk about the possibilities of seeing what you studied. Are any plants alive in this season?

3

Observe

Did you find what you were looking for? Why? Why not? Did you learn something from seeing this in creation?

CHECK LIST

- ☐ Worship
- ☐ Bible Reading
- ☐ Complete worksheets with each child
- ☐ Individual reading/reading out loud
- ☐ Math of choice

WEEK 3, DAY 4

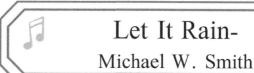

Let It Rain-
Michael W. Smith

Read to student:

*NOTE to parents: The goal of teaching the kings of Israel and Judah is to help your child grasp the narrative of the Bible, the ability to trace who Jesus was, and to follow the history of Israel. There are MANY FANTASTIC truths in Kings and Chronicles and also some hard lessons. We will read a couple of these incredible stories next week but essentially view this as a "layover" in Kings and Chronicles. As your child gets older, plan to spend more time on each of the kings and in these books.

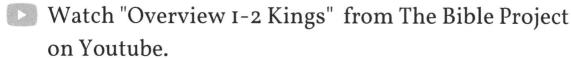

Watch "Overview 1-2 Kings" from The Bible Project on Youtube.

Please pray with your kids. Encourage them to pray also.

Scripture Memory Matthew 6:9-13

Scripture Memory 1 Samuel 12:24   Have your children say this with you.

"But be sure to fear the Lord and serve him faithfully with all your heart; consider what great things he has done for you."

✓ While you read the Bible, have your children color the picture on their handwriting sheet. Older children may help with the reading.

 Bible Reading: 1 Kings 1:28-3, 6:11-14

Have the student(s) tell back what you read. Offer help along the way and kindly explain what you expect when they tell back a story. Be encouraging and compliment them.

✓ Handwriting Project   *Third and up write from memory.

At the end of each week, have your student practice their best handwriting. Remove this sheet and share with a friend, family member, or persecuted/imprisoned Christian (send through Voice of the Martyrs). Have children 3rd and up address the envelope and write their return address.

Practical Learning

Have students repeat these facts after you. *Give practical examples and hands on demonstrations when possible and when needed.

- Say the Lord's Prayer.
- Volume is another way we know how much of something there is, or how much is needed. We use these often in recipes. There are 8 ounces in one cup, 2 cups in a pint, 2 pints in a quart, and 4 quarts in a gallon.

Read to student:

Give time for them to answer questions and remind them when needed.

Let's review what we have learned this week.

Can you tell me something we learned from the Bible?

Do you remember what a continent is?

✓ Review anything from this week that your children struggled with. (Examples: sight words, letters)

✓ Language Arts Section in Student Workbook

📖 Read out loud to your children. This is a great time to read historical books. Be sure to choose books that are written from a Christian perspective or audit them closely for anything that isn't God-glorifying and true.

✓ Spend a few minutes with each child checking in on their reading progress. Make sure older children are able to decode words in syllables. Make sure younger children are recognizing their sight words within the text of a book.

CHECK LIST

☐ Worship

☐ Bible Reading

☐ Complete worksheets with each child

☐ Individual reading/reading out loud

☐ Math of choice

WEEK 4, DAY 1

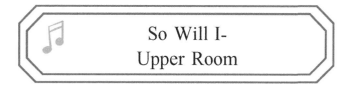

So Will I-
Upper Room

Read to student:

This is our last week of unit three! Can you tell me one thing you have learned in this unit? This is the week you get to choose your special country project.

The kingdom of Israel was only united by three kings before it split. Saul, David, and part of Solomon's reign were when all twelve tribes were united and ruled together. Partway through Solomon's reign the kingdom split into the northern and southern kingdoms. Ten tribes became the kingdom of Israel in the north, while Judah and Benjamin became the kingdom of Judah in the south. God sent prophets to speak to His people and to the kings. One of the most notable prophets was Elijah. Today we are going to read in the Bible about Elijah and hear some of the amazing miracles that God performed!

 Please pray with your kids. Encourage them to pray also.

Scripture Memory Matthew 6:9-13

Scripture Memory 1 Kings 18:37   Have your children say this with you.

"Answer me, Lord, answer me, so these people will know that you, Lord, are God, and that you are turning their hearts back again."

✓ While you read the Bible, have your kids color the picture on their handwriting sheet.

📖 Bible Reading: 1 Kings 17-19

Have the student(s) act out the story or a portion of the story that you read. Offer help with ideas and narration. You can make this as simple or complex as you wish.

 Handwriting practice

 Language Arts Section in Student Workbook

Review

- Tell me one of the 10 Commandments.
- Do you remember your memory verse from last week?
- Tell me one thing you are thankful for!

Read to student:

Isn't it amazing that God took care of Elijah the way He did? Always remember that Yahweh, the one true God, has power. All false gods and demonic forces of evil in the heavenly realms are nothing when compared with the Creator of the heavens and the earth! Our God is all-powerful and all-mighty. We can trust Yahweh to be faithful to us and answer our prayers when we call to Him just as He did for Elijah.

 For our art time today, we are going to spend time working on our individual handicrafts. I will be available to help you if you need something. The Bible tells us to work the best we can in all we are doing. I want you to do your best work. It is good when we have skills that we are able to share with others. As we practice, we get better at whatever we are working on! Don't get discouraged if you don't immediately catch on! You will get better the more you practice.

*Note to parents: Have your child work on skills that you chose for them at the beginning of the year. It is great to have them work on this more often than is built into our curriculum, however, every fourth week of our units will be a dedicated time to working on these.

 Read out loud to your children. This is a great time to read historical books. Be sure to choose books that are written from a Christian perspective or audit them closely for anything that isn't God-glorifying and true. Children grades 1-5 should also spend time reading age-appropriate books.

CHECK LIST

- ☐ Worship
- ☐ Bible Reading
- ☐ Art Project

- ☐ Individual reading/reading out loud
- ☐ Complete worksheets with each child
- ☐ Math of choice

♪ Give Me Jesus
Fernando Ortega

Read to student:

Elijah is one of two people (the other is Enoch found Genesis 5:21-24) the Bible does not record as having died. He was simply caught up to heaven, and the mantle of his anointing from God fell to Elisha. Elisha was filled with power from God and went about in Israel. The miracles that God used both Elijah and Elisha to perform are simply amazing. I hope that you always feel joy and awe over the miracles that God performs and that you always believe Him for Bible-level miracles in your life! He is still every bit as powerful now as He was when the Bible was written. The same God whose power rose Jesus from the grave lives in us through the Holy Spirit! (Romans 6:10-11)

 Please pray with your kids. Encourage them to pray also.

Scripture Memory Matthew 6:9-13   Found at the beginning of this unit.

Scripture Memory 1 Kings 18:37   Have your children say this with you.

"Answer me, Lord, answer me, so these people will know that you, Lord, are God, and that you are turning their hearts back again."

 While you read the Bible, have your kids color the picture on their handwriting sheet.

 Bible Reading: 2 Kings 2, 4-6

Have the student(s) tell back what you read. Offer help along the way and kindly explain what you expect when they tell back a story. Be encouraging and compliment them.

 Handwriting practice

Practical Learning Have students repeat these facts after you.

- There are 5,280 feet in a mile.
- What did Jesus say the greatest commandments are? (Matt. 22:37-39)
    1. Love the LORD your God with all your heart, soul, and strength
    2. The second is like it, love your neighbor as yourself.
        All of the Law and prophets hang on these two commands.

✓ Language Arts Section in Student Workbook

 Read to student:

Today it's time for a country project! Are you excited? Can you tell me why you chose the option you chose for our project? What is something that drew you to this country? Let's pray specifically for this country.
1. Pray for believers there to live for the Lord, love His Word, share the Gospel, and seek first the kingdom of God.
2. Pray for their government officials to come to know Jesus and to have the wisdom to wisely lead their people. Pray for freedom to worship Jesus and peace.
3. Pray for missionaries in this country and the leaders of God's people. Pray for safety and that they would not grow weary in doing good.
4. Pray for the Lord to send more gospel workers into the harvest. Jesus said the harvest is plentiful but the laborers few! (Matthew 9:35-38)

Note: Encourage your child to do their best on their project. Help when needed. Don't forget to have them present their project to a family member or friend.

✓ Geography Section in Student Workbook

Read out loud to your children, this is a great time to read historical books. Be sure to choose books that are written from a Christian perspective or audit them closely for anything that isn't God-glorifying and true. Children grades 1-5 should also spend time reading age-appropriate books.

CHECK LIST

- ☐ Worship
- ☐ Bible Reading
- ☐ Complete worksheets with each child
- ☐ Individual reading/reading out loud
- ☐ Math of choice

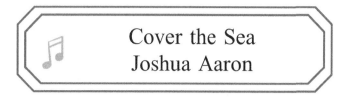

Cover the Sea
Joshua Aaron

Read to student:

We are going to read about a few of the kings who served God and led the people well. There are unique lessons we can learn from each of the kings. God did not allow anything into the Bible as a mistake or an accident. Even the kings who did not serve Yahweh tell a story we need to know- a sad story of what happens to those who do not fear the LORD.

I want you to notice how young Josiah was when he became king! Can you imagine being king at only eight years old? What a responsibility! Although he reigned so young, he is remembered as one of the best kings because he found out what God's Law said and obeyed it! Remember, although you are young, you can decide to obey God with your whole heart.

 Please pray with your kids. Encourage them to pray also.

Scripture Memory Matthew 6:9-13

Scripture Memory 1 Kings 18:37   Have your children say this with you.

"Answer me, Lord, answer me, so these people will know that you, Lord, are God, and that you are turning their hearts back again."

 While you read the Bible, have your kids color the picture on their handwriting sheet.

 Bible Reading: 2 Kings 18-20, 22-23

Have the student(s) tell back what you read. Offer help along the way and kindly explain what you expect when they tell back a story. Be encouraging and compliment them.

 Language Arts Section in Student Workbook

 # Science

We have spent the last couple of weeks learning about the plants that grow on the ground. Have you ever stopped to think about the soil that they grow in? Soil is made up of many different parts. Not all dry ground is suitable for growing plants. Since we are focused on what God created on the third day, we are going to spend time today learning more about types of soil! Jesus told a parable about what type of soil is best for growing seeds. Do you know this parable? Where do we not want to plant seeds? How do we know what good soil is? Let's learn!

✓ Science Worksheet

▶ Watch "Layers of Soil" from Peekaboo Kidz on Youtube.

EDDIBLE SOIL
SCIENCE ACTIVITY

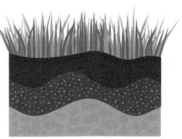

We are going to make edible soil layers!
Please look on lampandlightliving Unit 3 Pinterest board for the visual of how to layer and label each section.

You will need:

- Chocolate pudding
- Chocolate chips/PB chips
- Crushed chocolate crackers
- Green-colored coconut flakes
- Gummy worms (optional)

Discuss what you have learned about each layer as you create your treat. If a family member is available, have your child explain the treat and what each layer symbolizes, what layers have roots that grow into them, and why each layer is important.

Practical Learning

- Say the books of the Bible either from memory or with song.
- For students who are confident readers, have them do a couple of Sword Drills. Sword Drills are fun competitions to see how fast you can find something in the Bible. Psalm 100:1, 2 Kings 2:22, Galatians 5:19

 Language Arts Section in Student Workbook

 ## Observation Walk

Go on a walk outdoors and try to <u>observe</u> in creation what you <u>studied</u> in Science. Allow children to bring a notebook if they want to record their observations.
Use these three points to help start the discussion:

Look

Discuss what you are looking for. Find the location around your outdoor environment with the highest probability.

Factor

Talk about the possibilities of seeing what you studied. What layer of soil can you see?

Observe

Did you find what you were looking for? Why? Why not? Did you learn something from seeing this in creation?

CHECK LIST

- ☐ Worship
- ☐ Bible Reading
- ☐ Complete worksheets with each child
- ☐ Individual reading/reading out loud
- ☐ Math of choice

WEEK 4, DAY 4

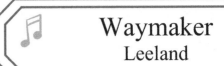
Read to student:

Today we are going to read an AMAZING story! Do you ever think of singing praise to God as battle or warfare? It is! God literally defeated the enemies of the Israelites because the Israelites praised Him. Sometimes we forget how important it is to praise God.

God desires our worship and praise. It truly is life-changing to understand that God can move in the spiritual realm when we don't even fully know what is happening. We can trust God to go with us always.

 Please pray with your kids. Encourage them to pray also.

Scripture Memory Matthew 6:9-13

Scripture Memory 1 Kings 18:37   Have your children say this with you.

"Answer me, Lord, answer me, so these people will know that you, Lord, are God, and that you are turning their hearts back again."

✓ **While you read the Bible, have your children color the picture on their handwriting sheet. Older children may help with the reading.**

📖 Bible Reading: 2 Chronicles 20

Have the student(s) tell back what you read. Offer help along the way and kindly explain what you expect when they tell back a story. Be encouraging and compliment.

✓ Handwriting Project   *Third and up write from memory.

At the end of each week, have your student practice their best handwriting. Remove this sheet and share with a friend, family member, or persecuted/imprisoned Christian (send through Voice of the Martyrs). Have children 3rd and up address the envelope and write their return address.

End of unit review:

Give time for them to answer questions and remind them when needed.

We are finished with our third unit of school! Wow! great job. I am enjoying teaching you and learning with you. Let's do a review of some of the things are have learned!

Can you tell me something we learned from the Bible?

Is there one verse or lesson that really helped you?
Did the LORD comfort or convict you in any area?

What is something you learned about land or plants?

Tell me a historical person you most enjoyed learning about. Why did you enjoy their story?

What was your favorite thing you learned about Asia?

✓ Review anything from this week that your children struggled with. (Examples: sight words, letters)

✓ Language Arts Section in Student Workbook

📖 Read out loud to your children, this is a great time to read historical books. Be sure to choose books that are written from a Christian perspective or audit them closely for anything that isn't God-glorifying and true.

✓ Spend a few minutes with each child checking in on their reading progress. Make sure older children are able to decode words into syllables. Make sure younger children are recognizing their sight words within the text of a book.

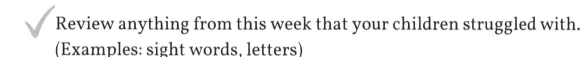

CHECK LIST

☐ Worship
☐ Bible Reading
☐ Complete worksheets with each child
☐ Individual reading/reading out loud
☐ Math of choice

Mini-Unit Study Plan

✓ Choose a topic

✓ Find needed resources- videos, websites, books

✓ Choose activities: field trip, experiment, movie

✓ Find Scriptures that many apply

1

Plan

Work with your child(ren) to come up with the best study for your family. Make a plan and allow them to be involved in finding resources and ideas.

2

Learn

Choose ways that learning will be involved. Examples include a write up, making lists, books to read, and more

3

Enjoy

Have fun! Allow your child to talk to others about their experience. Try to enjoy this week together and foster a desire to learn more.

WEEK 5 DAILY CHECK LIST

☐ Unit Study   ☐ Math of choice

☐ Unit Study   ☐ Math of choice

☐ Unit Study   ☐ Math of choice

☐ Unit Study   ☐ Math of choice

UNIT
Four

GOSPEL FOCUS & EYES ON JESUS

Here's your reminder that God gave you your children. He thought you would be the best person to teach them, train them, and guide them towards Himself. We can trust the Lord to teach our children better than we ever can. Our most important job as parents is to be absolutely certain, to the best of our abilities, that our children know Jesus as Lord, and are discipled in God's ways. If you feel weary, allow God to refresh your soul. Take a few minutes to be still and know that God is God, and He will be exalted in the heavens and on the earth.

PRAY

Pause and intentionally pray over your school time. Ask the Lord to work through the time you spend educating your children to give you and your children a kingdom first perspective. Ask the Lord to help you keep your eyes on Jesus. Seek the Lord for opportunities and ways you and your children can share the gospel and pray for anyone you have shared the gospel with. Pray for each of your children that they would know and serve the Lord.

QUESTIONS

1. Am I being intentional with our homeschool time?
2. Are we simply checking boxes or are my children learning to love Jesus and others through our schooling?
3. Do I feel burned out? If so, seek the Lord for new strength
4. How can I best use the time I have with my children? Are we too busy to focus on what matters most?
5. Have I let distractions creep into our day that we need to reduce?

EXTRA
Resources

UNIT VERSE

Blessed are the poor in spirit, for theirs is the kingdom of heaven.
Blessed are those who mourn, for they will be comforted.
Blessed are the meek, for they will inherit the earth.
Blessed are those who hunger and thirst for righteousness,
for they will be filled.
Blessed are the merciful, for they will be shown mercy.
Blessed are the pure in heart, for they will see God.
Blessed are the peacemakers, for they will be called children of
God.
Blessed are those who are persecuted because of righteousness,
for theirs is the kingdom of heaven.
Matthew 5:3-10

PRAYER REQUESTS

Record things you and your children would like to pray over here. Be sure to check
back and praise the Lord when He answers. Prompt your kids to think about praying
for others. Read Matthew 6:9-13 for how Jesus taught us to pray. As you study the
Word notice the pattern of Biblical prayers and prayer requests and try to learn from
the Word.

_____   _____

_____   _____

_____   _____

_____   _____

_____   _____

WEEK 1, DAY 1

🎵 Lover of My Soul- Kari Jobe

Read to student:

Welcome to our next unit! In unit four we will be studying Australia, the sun, the moon, and the stars. We also have an exciting art project we are going to work on in this unit for art. We are going to make a Bible story game!

For our Bible lessons, we will be moving to the New Testament and studying Jesus' life. We are going to read through the book of Luke. Instead of working on a weekly memory verse and a unit verse, we are going to memorize one longer passage of Scripture for this unit. We call these the beatitudes and they are found in Jesus' longest teaching, The Sermon on the Mount. Are you excited to learn about Jesus' life? Tell me some things you already know about Jesus!

 Please pray with your kids. Encourage them to pray also.

▶ Watch "Overview: New Testament" from The Bible Project on YouTube

Scripture Memory Matthew 5:3-10

✓ While you read the Bible, have your kids color their sheet in their workbook.

📖 Bible Reading: Luke 1

Have the student(s) tell back what you read. Offer help along the way and kindly explain what you expect when they tell back a story. Be encouraging and compliment them.

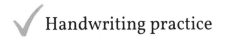 Handwriting practice

Review

- Say the ABCs
- (1st +) Do you remember what nouns and verbs are? (Noun- person, place, or thing. Verb- a word that shows action.)
- (1st +) When do we capitalize the first letter of a word? (Beginning of a sentence, proper noun, and the word I.)
- We are going to learn (practice) the calendar. Do you know how many days are in a week? How many months are in a year?
  Say the days of the week and the months of the year.

✓ Language Arts Section in Student Workbook

 Are you ready to create a Bible-themed game?
I would like you to choose between making your game based on the story of the Bible, or one specific Bible story. You will also need to choose what kind of game you would like to create. Think about your favorite game to play. Do you enjoy memory? Do you like trivia games? Or, perhaps card games?
Here are some ideas:
Bible Memory Cards
Bible Trivia
Re-create a game with a Bible theme: Bible Land, Bibleopoly, Bible Go Fish

We will work on this project for our art project for this unit so you will have four weeks to complete this project. Take your time and make it nice!

Read out loud to your children, this is a great time to read historical books. Be sure to choose books that are written from a Christian perspective or audit them closely for anything that isn't God-glorifying and true. Children grades 1-5 should also spend time reading age-appropriate books.

CHECK LIST

- ☐ Worship
- ☐ Bible Reading
- ☐ Art Project

- ☐ Individual reading/reading out loud
- ☐ Complete worksheets with each child
- ☐ Math of choice

WEEK 1, DAY 2

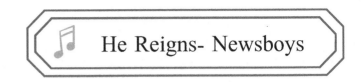

He Reigns- Newsboys

Read to student:

Today we are going to read about one of the most important events in history! The birth of Jesus Christ. Jesus was fully God and fully man. He was born for a specific purpose, a plan that God had since the foundation of the world. God knew we would need a Savior from our sins and Jesus was His plan, a way to come and redeem us. As we read this story, I want you to imagine what it would have been like to be there when Jesus was born. I want you to think about the smells, how it would look, who would be there, and how you would feel.

Today's chapter covers a big space of time! It goes all the way from when Jesus was born to when He was twelve years old. In all of those years and beyond, Jesus was learning, perhaps like you are right now. He was learning things like reading and writing, and most importantly the text of the Bible. Although He was God, He still had to learn on this earth!

 Please pray with your kids. Encourage them to pray also.

Scripture Memory Matthew 5:3-10

✓ While you read the Bible have your kids color their sheet in their workbook.

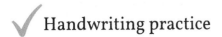 Bible Reading: Luke 2

Have the student(s) tell back what you read. Offer help along the way and kindly explain what you expect when they tell back a story. Be encouraging and compliment them.

✓ Handwriting practice

Practical Learning Have students repeat these facts after you.

- There are 24 hours in a day, 60 minutes in an hour, and 60 seconds in a minute.
- There are 52 weeks in a year and 7 days in a week.
- "Thirty days hath September, April, June, and November; all the rest have 31 except February which has 28, except on leap year when it has 29."
- There are 365 days in a year, leap year has 366.

Language Arts Section in Student Workbook

 Look at a globe or map with your child, and show them Australia/Oceania. Point out different countries and ask them to begin thinking about which country they would like to study more.

Read to student:

Today we are going to begin learning about Australia/Oceania. There are 14 countries in total, two of them being in Australia. There are over 10,000 islands that make up Oceania! The total population is over 43 million, with the most populated country being Australia.

 Read a continent book about Australia/Oceania.

Continent Study in Student Workbook

 Read out loud to your children, this is a great time to read historical books. Be sure to choose books that are written from a Christian perspective or audit them closely for anything that isn't God-glorifying and true. Children grades 1-5 should also spend time reading age-appropriate books.

CHECK LIST

- [ ] Worship
- [ ] Bible Reading
- [ ] Complete worksheets with each child
- [ ] Individual reading/reading out loud
- [ ] Math of choice

WEEK 1, DAY 3

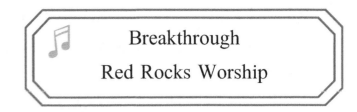

Breakthrough

Red Rocks Worship

Read to student:

When you hear "Prepare the way", what do you think of?

John the Baptist was to prepare the way for the Lord, Jesus! He went about preaching repentance and openly said he wasn't the Messiah.

Do you remember how John was related to Jesus? Yes, His cousin! All the way back before John was born, even while he was in his mother's belly, he knew Jesus. Even Jesus was baptized.

The Bible: the inspired Word of God Learn the books of the Bible to song

66 books make up one, big book

39 books in the OT, 27 books in the NT

 Please pray with your kids. Encourage them to pray also.

Scripture Memory Matthew 5:3-10

 While you read the Bible have your kids color their sheet in their workbook.

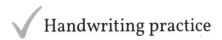 Bible Reading: Luke 3

Have the student(s) tell back what you read. Offer help along the way and kindly explain what you expect when they tell back a story. Be encouraging and compliment them.

Question: How old was Jesus when He began His ministry?

✓ Handwriting practice

Science

On the fourth day of creation, God spoke the sun, moon, and stars into existence. He said that He created the greater light to rule the day and the lesser light to rule the night. He also said He gave them for signs and seasons! Isn't that interesting? God's times and seasons revolve around His feast days, appointed times He wants to meet with His people. The sun and moon help us to keep time and to keep track of seasons, months, years, and hours. Did you know the moon has phases? The cycle of the moon is how we determine a month. The Bible talks about a celebration called the New Moon feast. A new moon is when the moon is totally dark before it starts its phases of visibility anew.

MOON PHASE
SCIENCE ACTIVITY

We will need:
- A way to observe the moon
- The moon phase chart from student workbooks

We are going to track the phase of the moon this month! Using your chart found in your workbook and observe the moon tonight and begin tracking. You will need to note that the moon is either waxing or waning.

Watch "Phases of the Moon: Astronomy and Space for Kids" from Free School on Youtube.

 Science Worksheet

Practical Learning Present these for your family and without causing your kids to feel afraid. They are wise things we must teach.

- What do we do in the event of a fire? *Also teach stop, drop, and roll
- What do we do in the event of a natural disaster *fill in with applicable events such as earthquakes, tornadoes, or other.
- Should you ever go with a stranger? NO! Even if they tell you that they know your mom and dad you need to run and immediately come find one of your parents.

 Language Arts Section in Student Workbook

 Observation Walk

Go on a walk outdoors and try to <u>observe</u> in creation what you <u>studied</u> in Science. Allow children to bring a notebook if they want to record their observations.
Use these three points to help start the discussion:

 1

Look

Discuss what you are looking for.
Go out at night if possible to view the moon.

 2

Factor

Talk about the possibilities of seeing what you studied. Is it cloudy or clear?

 3

Observe

Did you find what you were looking for? Why? Why not? Did you learn something from seeing this in creation?

CHECK LIST

- ☐ Worship
- ☐ Bible Reading
- ☐ Complete worksheets with each child
- ☐ Individual reading/reading out loud
- ☐ Math of choice

WEEK 1, DAY 4

♩ Protector

Kim Walker Smith

Read to student:

Let's play Bible trivia today! I am going to ask questions, you tell me the right answer as fast as you can. (In our family we offer chocolate chips or other small treats for correct answers. It makes Bible trivia extra sweet and the kids really enjoy it. If you are interested in more questions than are provided, download our free Bible trivia printable on www.lampandlightmerchandise.com)

Bible Trivia

1. What day did God create the sun, moon, and stars?
2. Who baptized Jesus?
3. How old was Jesus when He began His ministry?
4. What was Jesus' mom's name?
5. Name one king of Israel.
6. How many loaves and fish did Jesus use to multiply to feed the people?
7. What was Jesus' first public miracle?
8. How can we be saved?

 Please pray with your kids. Encourage them to pray also.

Scripture Memory Matthew 5:3-10

 While you read the Bible have your children color the picture on their handwriting sheet. Older children may help with the reading.

 Bible Reading: Luke 4

Have the student(s) tell back what you read. Offer help along the way and kindly explain what you expect when they tell back a story. Be encouraging and compliment them.

✓ Handwriting Project   *Third and up write from memory.

At the end of each week have your student practice their best handwriting. Remove this sheet and share with a friend, family member, or persecuted/imprisoned Christian (send through Voice of the Martyrs). Have children 3rd and up address the envelope and write their return address.

Practical Learning

Have students repeat these facts after you. *Give practical examples and hands on demonstrations when possible and when needed.

- Say the Armor of God (Helmet of salvation, the breastplate of righteousness, the belt of truth, feet shod with the readiness of the gospel of peace, shield of faith, sword of the Spirit which is the Word of God.
- Measurement is broken down into units. An inch is a common unit of measurement. There are 12 inches in a foot, and 3 feet in a yard.

✓ Review anything from this week that your children struggled with. (Examples: Sight words, letters)

✓ Language Arts Section in Student Workbook

📖 Read out loud to your children, this is a great time to read historical books. Be sure to choose books that are written from a Christian perspective or audit them closely for anything that isn't God glorifying and true. Children grades 1-5 should also spend time reading age-appropriate books.

CHECK LIST

- ☐ Worship
- ☐ Bible Reading
- ☐ Complete worksheets with each child
- ☐ Individual reading/reading out loud
- ☐ Math of choice

WEEK 2, DAY 1

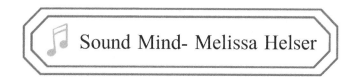

Read to student:

Today we are going to watch a Bible video about Luke chapters 1-9. Sometimes it is helpful to have an overview of what you are studying!

Hint: Notice what the video says about Luke being a two-part work- Part two is what we will study for our next unit!

▶ Watch "Overview: Luke 1-9" from The Bible Project on YouTube

 Please pray with your kids. Encourage them to pray also.

Scripture Memory Matthew 5:3-10

Tip: This week provide the first portion of each beatitude and see if your child(ren) can fill in the second part. For example: "Blessed are the pure in heart"....

✓ While you read the Bible have your kids color the picture on their handwriting sheet.

📖 Bible Reading: Luke 5

Spend a few minutes discussing what happens when people don't follow God. Try to ask your children thought-provoking questions about the difference between obeying rules that are for our good versus disobeying.

✓ Handwriting practice

✓ Language Arts Section in Student Workbook

Review + Focus

- What continent did we study in our last unit? Tell me one fact about it!
- How would you share the gospel with someone? Start with telling them who Jesus is. (Help as needed, encourage your kids to use what they practice to really share about Jesus with kids they encounter in your neighborhood, at the park, or otherwise.)
- Tell me one prayer that God has answered for you!
- Tell me one thing you are thankful for!

 Art Project:

Continue work on your Bible game

Work the best you can on your game! If you construct this game well, it will be fun to play with your friends and family!

Read out loud to your children, this is a great time to read historical books. Be sure to choose books that are written from a Christian perspective or audit them closely for anything that isn't God-glorifying and true. Children grades 1-5 should also spend time reading age-appropriate books.

CHECK LIST

☐ Worship

☐ Bible Reading

☐ Art Project

☐ Individual reading/reading out loud

☐ Complete worksheets with each child

☐ Math of choice

WEEK 2, DAY 2

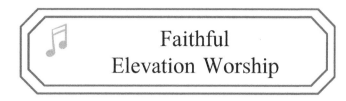
Faithful
Elevation Worship

Read to student:

Jesus is our Savior but He also was a great teacher! He performed many miracles and explained the Scriptures to the people. Today you will hear Luke's account of portions of the Sermon on the Mount. Listen for the section that sounds similar to our memory verse! Matthew 5-7 is the longest continuous dialogue of Jesus that is recorded in Scripture. It is important to remember that the Gospels are four different people's accounts of the same story.

 Please pray with your kids. Encourage them to pray also.

Scripture Memory Matthew 5:3-10

 While you read the Bible have your kids color the picture on their handwriting sheet.

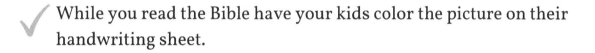 Bible Reading: Luke 6

Have the student(s) tell back what you read. Offer help along the way and kindly explain what you expect when they tell back a story. Be encouraging and compliment them.

Question:
What did the wise man build his house upon?
What did this symbolize?

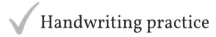 Handwriting practice

Practical Learning Have students repeat these facts after you.

- A penny is worth 1 cent, a nickel is worth 5 cents, a dime is worth 10 cents, and a quarter is worth 25 cents.
- There are 100 cents in a dollar.
- For older kids, challenge them to tell you what amount of money different combinations of coins make.

 Language Arts Section in Student Workbook

 Read to student:

Do you remember what you learned last week about Australia/Oceania? Today we are going to have some fun with what we learned! We are going to make the information you learned into a visual report that you can share with others. There is a sheet in your workbook to help you get started.

Things to consider encouraging your child to add:
- Visual appeal with colors, themes, and facts
- Stickers, printed or magazine images, or drawings
- Number of countries
- Top natural resources
- Main religion, percent of known Christians *Be sure to share that this isn't always accurate if a country has laws against Christianity. We could have brothers and sisters in Christ not openly declaring their religion.
- Main bodies of water
- Any significant landmarks- both natural and man-made

 Read out loud to your children, this is a great time to read historical books. Be sure to choose books that are written from a Christian perspective or audit them closely for anything that isn't God-glorifying and true. Children grades 1-5 should also spend time reading age-appropriate books.

CHECK LIST

- ☐ Worship
- ☐ Bible Reading
- ☐ Complete worksheets with each child
- ☐ Individual reading/reading out loud
- ☐ Math of choice

WEEK 2, DAY 3

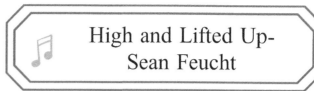
Read to student:

How was Jesus different than any other human that has ever lived?
Jesus lived perfectly and He showed humility and compassion that is simply astounding. He turned the world upside down forever with His teachings. There has never been and there never will be anyone else like Jesus! He is the perfect example and lived out everything He taught. As we continue to read about Jesus I want you to think about how you can be like Jesus.

▶ Watch "The Baptism of Jesus Luke 3-9" from The Bible Project on YouTube

🙏 Please pray with your kids. Encourage them to pray also.

Scripture Memory Matthew 5:3-10   Found at the beginning of this unit.

✓ While you read the Bible have your kids color the picture on their handwriting sheet.

📖 Bible Reading: Luke 7

Have the student(s) tell back what you read. Offer help along the way and kindly explain what you expect when they tell back a story. Be encouraging and compliment them.

✓ Handwriting practice

 Science

We are going to learn about stars today! Can you tell me a very important star in the Bible? In the book of Matthew, a very special star is recorded when Jesus was born. Let's read about it! READ: Matthew 2:1-12

Science tells us that the sun is a star, but it is important to remember that the Bible doesn't say that. The Bible is straightforward when it speaks about the sun as the greater light that rules the day. It is important that we always test what we learn to what we already know from the Bible. We always can believe the Bible!

 Watch "Constellations: Connect the Dots in the Sky?" from SciShowKids on Youtube.

✓ Science Worksheet and Experiment

 CONSTELLATIONS
SCIENCE ACTIVITY

We are going to see how many constellations we can find!

We will need:
- A clear night sky
- Grapes
- Toothpicks

- Find at least one constellation
- Construct the constellation out of toothpicks and grapes
- Share your constellation creations with your family and tell them how many constellations you were able to locate.

Practical Learning

Present these for your family and without causing your kids to feel afraid. They are wise things we must teach.

- What do we do in the event of a fire? *Also teach stop, drop, and roll
- What do we do in the event of a natural disaster *fill in with applicable events such as earthquakes, tornadoes, or other.
- Should you ever go with a stranger? NO! Even if they tell you that they know your mom and dad you need to run and immediately come to find one of your parents.

 Language Arts Section in Student Workbook

 ## Observation Walk

Go on a walk outdoors and try to <u>observe</u> in creation what you <u>studied</u> in Science. Allow children to bring a notebook if they want to record their observations.
Use these three points to help start the discussion:

1	**2**	**3**
## Look	## Factor	## Observe
Discuss what you are looking for. Find the location around your outdoor environment with the highest probability.	Talk about the possibilities of seeing what you studied. Is it clear or cloudy?	Did you find what you were looking for? Why? Why not? Did you learn something from seeing this in creation?

CHECK LIST

- ☐ Worship
- ☐ Bible Reading
- ☐ Complete worksheets with each child
- ☐ Individual reading/reading out loud
- ☐ Math of choice

WEEK 2, DAY 4

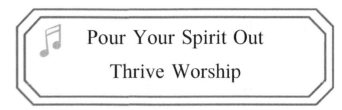
Read to student:

Disciples were people who followed Jesus and learned from Him. They wanted to be like Jesus and they knew that to be like Jesus they had to know Him very well!

Do you want to be a disciple of Jesus? The best thing we can do to be disciples of Jesus is to read about His life and be filled with the Holy Spirit who can lead us into Christlike action. As we read today I want you to listen carefully to the kinds of soil, and which kind produced a good harvest. Before we begin reading, let's pray that we will have good soil in our hearts for God's Word to grow and produce a good harvest within our lives!

 Please pray with your kids. Encourage them to pray also.

Scripture Memory Matthew 5:3-10

✓ While you read the Bible have your children color the picture on their handwriting sheet. Older children may help with the reading.

📖 Bible Reading: Luke 8

Have the student(s) tell back what you read. Offer help along the way and kindly explain what you expect when they tell back a story. Be encouraging and compliment.

✓ Handwriting Project   *Third and up write from memory.

At the end of each week have your student practice their best handwriting. Remove this sheet and share with a friend, family member, or persecuted/imprisoned Christian (send through Voice of the Martyrs). Have children 3rd and up address the envelope and write their return address.

Practical Learning

Have students repeat these facts after you. *Give practical examples and hands-on demonstrations when possible and when needed.

- Say the fruits of the Spirit: love, joy, peace, patience, kindness, goodness, faithfulness, gentleness, and self-control.
- Weight is how we know how heavy something is. An ounce is a small unit of weight. There are 16 ounces in a pound.

Read to student:

Give time for them to answer questions and remind them when needed.

Let's review what we have learned this week.
Can you tell me something we learned from the Bible?
Tell me one fact about Australia/Oceania.

 Review anything from this week that your children struggled with. (Examples: sight words, letters)

 Language Arts Section in Student Workbook

 Read out loud to your children. This is a great time to read historical books. Be sure to choose books that are written from a Christian perspective or audit them closely for anything that isn't God-glorifying and true. Children grades 1-5 should also spend time reading age-appropriate books.

 Help your child with their worksheet and report about a historical figure.

If you have not completed a book about a historical figure do your best to help your child find a historical person of interest to use for this exercise. Add words your child may struggle with when writing to next week's spelling list.

CHECK LIST

- [ ] Worship
- [ ] Bible Reading
- [ ] Complete worksheets with each child
- [ ] Individual reading/reading out loud
- [ ] Math of choice

WEEK 3, DAY 1

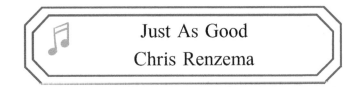
♫ Just As Good
Chris Renzema

Read to student:

Following Jesus isn't always easy, but it is worth it!

If Jesus called you what would your response be? Would you have other things you needed to do first, or would you follow Jesus?

What if Jesus asked you who He is? What would you say?

Peter answered correctly! He said Jesus was the Messiah. The Messiah had been prophesied to come for hundreds of years. Peter was raised to watch for Jesus. Did you know we are watching for Jesus too? We are watching for His second coming! We must be prepared, living obedient lives, obeying God's Word, and being faithful to Jesus' instructions so we are well prepared for when Jesus returns suddenly.

 Please pray with your kids. Encourage them to pray also.

Scripture Memory Matthew 5:3-10

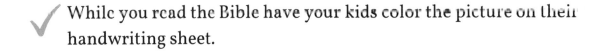 While you read the Bible have your kids color the picture on their handwriting sheet.

📖 Bible Reading: Luke 9

Have the student(s) act out the story or a portion of the story that you read. Offer help with ideas and narration. You can make this as simple or complex as you wish.

 Handwriting practice

 Language Arts Section in Student Workbook

Review

- How many days did it take God to create the world?
- Tell me the continents we have studied so far.
- Do you remember your memory verse from last week?
- Tell me one thing you are thankful for!

 Continue working on your Bible game project.

- Consider how you will store your game and make sure you have an idea worked out for storage.
- Do you need any standing pieces for your game? Consider constructing these from clay.
- Will you need anything like a sand timer or dice? Purchase these if so.

Read out loud to your children. This is a great time to read historical books. Be sure to choose books that are written from a Christian perspective or audit them closely for anything that isn't God-glorifying and true. Children grades 1-5 should also spend time reading age-appropriate books.

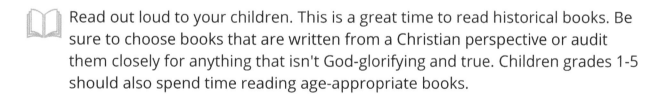

CHECK LIST

- ☐ Worship
- ☐ Bible Reading
- ☐ Art Project
- ☐ Individual reading/reading out loud
- ☐ Complete worksheets with each child
- ☐ Math of choice

WEEK 3, DAY 2

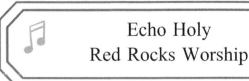

Read to student:

Jesus said the most important commandments are to love the LORD our God with all of our heart, soul, and strength AND to love our neighbor as ourselves. In today's reading, we learn who our neighbor is. Our neighbor is even our enemy!

The Samaritans and the Jews did not get along. The Jewish people thought the Samaritans were less than because they were mixed with the nations. Jesus Himself acknowledged the Jews were the ones who worshipped rightly (John 4:22). However, when it came to loving a neighbor Jesus told a parable with the Samaritan man as the one who knew how to love rightly. This parable must have greatly surprised His audience! It is so important for us to love even those who do wrong to us.

 Please pray with your kids. Encourage them to pray also.

▶ Watch "Overview: Luke 10-24" from The Bible Project on YouTube

Scripture Memory Matthew 5:3-10

✓ While you read the Bible have your kids color the picture on their handwriting sheet.

📖 Bible Reading: Luke 10

Have the student(s) tell back what you read. Offer help along the way and kindly explain what you expect when they tell back a story. Be encouraging and compliment them.

✓ Handwriting practice

Practical Learning Have students repeat these facts after you.

- Freezing temperature of water is 32 degrees F.
- Boiling temperature of water is 212 degrees F.
- Water expands when it freezes.
- Water can be in different forms. It can be a liquid, a solid (ice), and a gas (steam).

✓ Language Arts Section in Student Workbook

 Read to student:

Today we are going to study one country from Oceania. If you have not already done so, please choose a country to study. We are going to work together to find the answers to the questions on your worksheet. Next week we will choose a project to do for the country you chose. You will have different options to choose from. You may look ahead in your book now and decide which project you will do. While we study, we will look for information to prepare for next week.
Every country is unique. They have distinct features both geographically and culturally. Some countries are very diverse. Take the United States for example.- There are different areas of the United States that have very different cultures. How we talk even sounds a little bit different! In certain areas, the unique styles of food vary, the climate varies, and the natural resources and job opportunities vary. While there is variation within a country, a country shares a common government, currency (money), main language, and laws.

 Read out loud to your children. This is a great time to read historical books. Be sure to choose books that are written from a Christian perspective or audit them closely for anything that isn't God-glorifying and true. Children grades 1-5 should also spend time reading age-appropriate books.

CHECK LIST

- ☐ Worship
- ☐ Bible Reading
- ☐ Complete worksheets with each child
- ☐ Individual reading/reading out loud
- ☐ Math of choice

WEEK 3, DAY 3

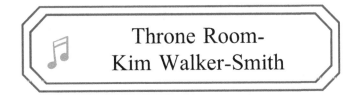

Throne Room-
Kim Walker-Smith

Read to student:

What would happen if we took half the walls away from our house? Yep, it would probably fall down. What about if the people inside of the house were divided? Do you think things would be pretty messy? What if your mom and dad never agreed? Not much would be accomplished!

Today in our reading we will hear Jesus talk about kingdoms being divided against themselves. Just like a house needs a foundation and walls to stand, God's kingdom cannot be divided. Beelzebul is another name for Satan or the Devil. Jesus could not be from the Devil because He was casting him out of people. The religious leaders were looking for any way to accuse Jesus. They didn't even bother to care if it made sense! Jesus was quickly able to refute their accusation because it was plain for everyone to see that He was doing good and was overcoming the Evil One.

 Please pray with your kids. Encourage them to pray also.

Scripture Memory Matthew 5:3-10

✓ While you read the Bible have your kids color the picture on their handwriting sheet.

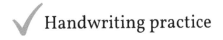 Bible Reading: Luke 11

Have the student(s) tell back what you read. Offer help along the way and kindly explain what you expect when they tell back a story. Be encouraging and compliment them.

✓ Handwriting practice

 # Science

So far in this unit, we have learned about the moon and stars. Are you remembering to track the phases of the moon? Today we are going to focus on the sun! I am certain you already know this, but the sun is VERY important. It provides heat for the earth, vitamin D, and food for plants to grow. God positioned the earth just at the right distance from the sun. If we were closer everything would burn up, if we were further away everything would freeze. What an amazing God we serve!

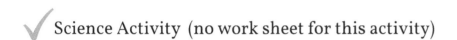 ## ▶ Watch "What is the Sun?" from SciShow Kids on Youtube.

✓ Science Activity (no work sheet for this activity)

SUN TO SCALE
SCIENCE ACTIVITY

You will need:

- Playdough (a few containers)
- A teaspoon
- A one-cup measuring cup
- Measuring tape

Directions:
As the video suggests we are going to make a to-scale model of the sun and the earth. The sun is roughly 100 times wider than the earth. To show this example we are going to use playdough and measure a 1 teaspoon-sized circle for the earth. Since 100 teaspoons are roughly 2 cups, we are going to measure roughly 2 cups to represent the sun.
The sun is roughly 94.5 million miles from the earth. We are going to scale the distance also so you will have a visual. We are going to say 1 inch represents 1 million miles. So, once your playdough models are finished, please measure 94.5 inches and place your models this distance apart. Can you imagine how big the sun really is?!

Practical Learning

- Each of the 50 states has a capital city. The capital of our state_____
- Washington D.C. is the capital of the United States.
- There are 12 tribes of Israel.
- Jesus had 12 disciples.

 Language Arts Section in Student Workbook

 Observation Walk

Go on a walk outdoors and try to <u>observe</u> in creation what you <u>studied</u> in Science. Allow children to bring a notebook if they want to record their observations.
Use these three points to help start the discussion:

1 Look

Discuss what you are looking for. Find the location around your outdoor environment with the highest probability.

2 Factor

Talk about the possibilities of seeing what you studied. Is the sun shining? Can you feel its warmth?

3 Observe

Did you find what you were looking for? Why? Why not? Did you learn something from seeing this in creation?

CHECK LIST

☐ Worship

☐ Bible Reading

☐ Complete worksheets with each child

☐ Individual reading/reading out loud

☐ Math of choice

WEEK 3, DAY 4

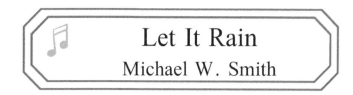
Read to student:

Trusting God for what we need can be challenging. It takes faith to believe that God will provide for our needs. Can you tell me a time when God provided something for you? Jesus said not to worry about things of this earth like clothes and food. He reminded the people that God already knows our needs and that we can be generous and seek first His kingdom instead of storing our treasures here.

It can be very tempting to want to hang onto what we have and not to share. Again and again, we are encouraged to be generous. How can you be generous? What do you have that you could share with others? Sometimes an ability is what we have! Maybe you are able to help someone in your family with a chore or a task. Maybe you can clean, watch younger kids, or do the dishes for your mom. Our time is valuable and it counts as something we can choose to share!

 Please pray with your kids. Encourage them to pray also.

Scripture Memory Matthew 5:3-10   Found at the beginning of this unit.

 While you read the Bible have your children color the picture on their handwriting sheet. Older children may help with the reading.

Bible Reading: Luke 12

Have the student(s) tell back what you read. Offer help along the way and kindly explain what you expect when they tell back a story. Be encouraging and compliment them.

✓ Handwriting Project   *Third and up write from memory.

At the end of each week have your student practice their best handwriting. Remove this sheet and share with a friend, family member, or persecuted/imprisoned Christian (send through Voice of the Martyrs). Have children 3rd and up address the envelope and write their return address.

Practical Learning

Have students repeat these facts after you. *Give practical examples and hands-on demonstrations when possible and when needed.

- Say the Lord's Prayer.
- Volume is another way we know how much of something there is, or how much is needed. we use these often in recipes. There are 8 ounces in one cup, 2 cups in a pint, 2 pints in a quart, and 4 quarts in a gallon.

Read to student:

Give time for them to answer questions and remind them when needed.

Let's review what we have learned this week.

Can you tell me something we learned from the Bible?

Tell me one fact about the sun, moon, or stars that you have learned.

✓ Review anything from this week that your children struggled with. (Examples: sight words, letters)

✓ Language Arts Section in Student Workbook

📖 Read out loud to your children. This is a great time to read historical books. Be sure to choose books that are written from a Christian perspective or audit them closely for anything that isn't God-glorifying and true.

✓ Spend a few minutes with each child checking in on their reading progress. Make sure older children are able to decode words in syllables. Make sure younger children are recognizing their sight words within the text of a book.

CHECK LIST

- [ ] Worship
- [ ] Bible Reading
- [ ] Complete worksheets with each child
- [ ] Individual reading/reading out loud
- [ ] Math of choice

WEEK 4, DAY 1

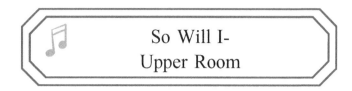
Read to student:

Can you tell me one thing you have learned in this unit? What is your favorite activity we have done so far during this unit?

Are you familiar with yeast? Do you know how much yeast is used for each cup of flour when making bread? The ratio is about the same as the sunshine-to-earth ratio we worked on last week! Just a small amount of yeast is used to work through a whole lot of flour. Jesus said that the kingdom of God is the same way! If we will share the kingdom of God it can produce a major result! Kingdom first mindset works into every part of our lives and changes everything!

Optional: Bake a loaf of homemade bread with your child(ren) to illustrate how yeast works.

 Please pray with your kids. Encourage them to pray also.

Scripture Memory Matthew 5:3-10   Found at the beginning of this unit.

 While you read the Bible have your kids color the picture on their handwriting sheet.

 Bible Reading: Luke 13

Have the student(s) act out the story or a portion of the story that you read. Offer help with ideas and narration. You can make this as simple or complex as you wish.

 Handwriting practice

 Language Arts Section in Student Workbook

Review

- Tell me one of the 10 Commandments.
- Do you remember your memory verse from last week?
- Tell me one thing you are thankful for!

 Today we will finish our Bible games! It has been so much fun to work on this project with you. Thank you for doing your best work.
When you finish your project completely I would like to play the game you created with you.

Optional, but encouraged:
Host a special game evening. This can be with your immediate family or with friends. Make special snacks and play your child's game with them. Allow them to share about the process of making their game and why they chose the theme that they did.

Read out loud to your children. This is a great time to read historical books. Be sure to choose books that are written from a Christian perspective or audit them closely for anything that isn't God-glorifying and true. Children grades 1-5 should also spend time reading age-appropriate books.

CHECK LIST

- [ ] Worship
- [ ] Bible Reading
- [ ] Art Project

- [ ] Individual reading/reading out loud
- [ ] Complete worksheets with each child
- [ ] Math of choice

WEEK 4, DAY 2

Give Me Jesus -
Fernando Ortega

Read to student:

If you were invited to a really awesome party would you want to go?
That is what heaven is like! Better than the very best party we can ever think of! Many people make excuses for why they do not want to go to the place that Jesus is preparing. It is really sad. We want to spend eternity with Jesus, and we want to tell many people about Jesus!

Have you ever lost something that you looked for extensively? Jesus says we are something He looks for in that way. If we wander into sin, Jesus searches for us and all of heaven rejoices when we repent! Rather than remaining angry over our sins, God shows mercy, compassion, and joy over people who turn to Him. He celebrates!
Have you repented for your sin? It is the most important decision we will ever make!

 Please pray with your kids. Encourage them to pray also.

Scripture Memory Matthew 5:3-10

✓ While you read the Bible, have your kids color the picture on their handwriting sheet.

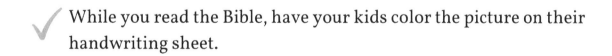 Bible Reading: Luke 14-15

Have the student(s) tell back what you read. Offer help along the way and kindly explain what you expect when they tell back a story. Be encouraging and compliment them.

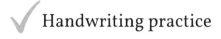 Handwriting practice

Practical Learning Have students repeat these facts after you.

- There are 5,280 feet in a mile.
- What did Jesus say the greatest commandments are? (Matt.
  1. Love the LORD your God with all your heart, soul, and strength
  2. The second is like it, love your neighbor as yourself.
     All of the Law and prophets hang on these two commands.

✓ Language Arts Section in Student Workbook

 Read to student:

Today we get to do our country project! Are you excited? Can you tell me why you chose the option you chose for our project? What is something that drew you to this country? Let's pray specifically for this country:
1. Pray for believers there to live for the Lord, love His Word, share the gospel, and seek first the kingdom of God.
2. Pray for their government officials to come to know Jesus and to have the wisdom to wisely lead their people. Pray for freedom to worship Jesus and peace.
3. Pray for missionaries in this country and leaders of God's people. Pray for safety and that they would not grow weary in doing good.
4. Pray for the Lord to send more gospel workers into the harvest. Jesus said the harvest is plentiful but the laborers few! (Matthew 9:35-38)

Note: Don't forget to have them present their project to a family member or friend.

✓ Geography Section in Student Workbook

Read out loud to your children. This is a great time to read historical books. Be sure to choose books that are written from a Christian perspective or audit them closely for anything that isn't God-glorifying and true. Children grades 1-5 should also spend time reading age-appropriate books.

CHECK LIST

- ☐ Worship
- ☐ Bible Reading
- ☐ Complete worksheets with each child
- ☐ Individual reading/reading out loud
- ☐ Math of choice

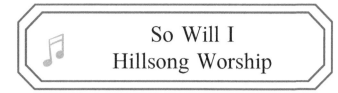

♫ So Will I
Hillsong Worship

Read to student:

Has something ever happened that wasn't what you expected? Maybe a bike ride that ended in an injury, a party you got sick at, or any other event that didn't happen the way you hoped or envisioned.

That is what Jesus was to the Jewish people. He was not what they expected and what they were watching for. He fulfilled all of the prophecies He needed to, yet they expected Him to come for the first time in power and destruction of their enemies. But He didn't. He came humble and lowly, yet great and mighty. Unlike an event that goes wrong, Jesus set everything right with His unexpected life. He taught humility that God had long valued and showed that the foolishness of man's wisdom is nothing when compared with the wisdom of God.

▶ Watch "Parables of Jesus" from The Bible Project on Youtube.

 Please pray with your kids. Encourage them to pray also.

Scripture Memory Matthew 5:3-10   Found at the beginning of this unit.

✓ While you read the Bible have your kids color the picture on their handwriting sheet.

📖 Bible Reading: Luke 16-17

Have the student(s) tell back what you read. Offer help along the way and kindly explain what you expect when they tell back a story. Be encouraging and compliment them.

✓ Language Arts Section in Student Workbook

 # Science

We've learned about the sun, moon, and stars. Today we are going to place them in our solar system and learn about the Milky Way Galaxy. The universe is how we describe everything- all of space and substance. Within the universe, there are many galaxies. Within the scientific community, you will find many that do not agree with the Biblical account of creation when studying the universe and galaxies. (I encourage looking up Answers in Genesis "How Old is the Earth?" for a Christian worldview on the age of the earth. Consider having older students read this article.) This is important to remember and to always choose the truth in the Bible.

Our focus today is going to be on the Milky Way Galaxy since this is where the earth is located! A galaxy is a huge collection of stars held together by gravitational attraction. Our solar system is within the Milky Way and includes the planets that orbit the sun. There are 8 planets total, including earth. Today we are going to learn about these!

▶ Watch "Exploring Our Solar System: Planets and Space for Kids" from Free School on Youtube.

✓ Science Worksheet

SOLAR SYSTEM
SCIENCE ACTIVITY

You will need:

- Sugar cookie dough
- Round cookie cutters (or lids to cut the dough)
- Icing
- Optional: food coloring

Directions:
Bake cookies and decorate to reflect the planets in our solar system.

Check out Lampandlightliving Unit 4 Pinterest board for visuals.

Practical Learning

- Say the books of the Bible either from memory or with song.
- For students that are confident readers have them do a couple of Sword Drills. Sword Drills are fun competitions to see how fast you can find something in the Bible. Ephesians 4:2, Revelation 1:7-8

 Language Arts Section in Student Workbook

 Observation Walk

Go on a walk outdoors and try to <u>observe</u> in creation what you <u>studied</u> in Science. Allow children to bring a notebook if they want to record their observations.
Use these three points to help start the discussion:

Look

Discuss what you are looking for.
Do you have access to a telescope?
Look up planets visible in your area.

Factor

Talk about the possibilities of seeing what you studied.

Observe

Did you find what you were looking for? Why? Why not?
Did you learn something from seeing this in creation?

CHECK LIST

- [ ] Worship
- [ ] Bible Reading
- [ ] Complete worksheets with each child
- [ ] Individual reading/reading out loud
- [ ] Math of choice

WEEK 4, DAY 4

Read to student:

Jesus loves and receives children. Even when others wanted to keep the children away from Jesus, Jesus called the children to Himself. Jesus told the adults to become like children in the way they receive the Kingdom of God! Does that make you feel honored?

Note: If you own the children's book "Kingdom Parables" you may wish to read the story of the persistent widow from this book to go along with Luke 18.

 Please pray with your kids. Encourage them to pray also.

Scripture Memory Matthew 5:3-10

 While you read the Bible have your children color the picture on their handwriting sheet. Older children may help with the reading.

Bible Reading: Luke 18

Have the student(s) tell back what you read. Offer help along the way and kindly explain what you expect when they tell back a story. Be encouraging and compliment.

Note: We will finish the book of Luke in our next unit.

Questions:
What did Jesus tell the rich young ruler to do if he wanted eternal life?
What healing is recorded in this chapter? What did the man do after he was healed?

Handwriting Project   *Third and up write from memory.

At the end of each week have your student practice their best handwriting. Remove this sheet and share with a friend, family member, or persecuted/imprisoned Christian (send through Voice of the Martyrs). Have children 3rd and up address the envelope and write their return address.

End of unit review:

Give time for them to answer questions and remind them when needed.

Wow! Great job this week! I am enjoying teaching you and learning with you. Let's do a review of some of the things we have learned through this unit!

Can you tell me something we learned from the Bible?

Is there one verse or lesson that really helped you?
Did the LORD comfort or convict you in any area?

What is something you learned about the sun, moon, and stars?

Tell me a historical person you most enjoyed learning about. Why did you enjoy their story?

What was your favorite thing you learned about Australia/Oceania?

✓ Review anything from this week that your children struggled with. (Examples: sight words, letters)

✓ Language Arts Section in Student Workbook

📖 Read out loud to your children. This is a great time to read historical books. Be sure to choose books that are written from a Christian perspective or audit them closely for anything that isn't God-glorifying and true.

✓ Spend a few minutes with each child checking in on their reading progress. Make sure older children are able to decode words into syllables. Make sure younger children are recognizing their sight words within the text of a book.

CHECK LIST

☐ Worship   ☐ Individual reading/reading out loud

☐ Bible Reading   ☐ Math of choice

☐ Complete worksheets with each child

WEEK 5

Mini-Unit Study Plan

✓ Choose a topic

✓ Find needed resources- videos, websites, books

✓ Choose activities: field trip, experiment, movie

✓ Find Scriptures that may apply

1

Plan

Work with your child(ren) to come up with the best study for your family. Make a plan and allow them to be involved in finding resources and ideas.

2

Learn

Choose ways that learning will be involved. Examples include a write up, making lists, books to read, and more

3

Enjoy

Have fun! Allow your child to talk to others about their experience. Try to enjoy this week together and foster a desire to learn more.

WEEK 5 DAILY CHECK LIST

☐ Unit Study   ☐ Math of choice

☐ Unit Study   ☐ Math of choice

☐ Unit Study   ☐ Math of choice

☐ Unit Study   ☐ Math of choice

UNIT
Five

GOSPEL FOCUS & EYES ON JESUS

Children learn much by what they see and do. We must model the actions we want them to imitate. We must put into practice what we learn. As the book of James says, we cannot only be hearers of the Word, we must be doers of the Word. Consider the actions in your family. Are there places that improvement is needed? It can be easy in our self-focused culture to forget to serve others and think more highly of ourselves than of others, yet these are Biblical truths. How can you be less focused on yourself? In what ways could you and your children serve someone else?

PRAY

Pause and intentionally pray over your school time. Ask the Lord to work through the time you spend educating your children to give you and your children a kingdom first perspective. Ask the Lord to help you keep your eyes on Jesus. Seek the Lord for opportunities and ways you and your children can share the gospel and pray for anyone you have shared the gospel with. Pray for each of your children that they would know and serve the Lord.

QUESTIONS

1. Am I being intentional with our homeschool time?
2. Are we simply checking boxes or are my children learning to love Jesus and others through our schooling?
3. Do I feel burned out? If so, seek the Lord for new strength
4. How can I best use the time I have with my children? Are we too busy to focus on what matters most?
5. Have I let distractions creep into our day that we need to reduce?

EXTRA
Resources

UNIT VERSE

"The Lord is my shepherd, I lack nothing. He makes me lie down in green pastures, he leads me beside quiet waters, he refreshes my soul. He guides me along the right paths for his name's sake. Even though I walk through the darkest valley, I will fear no evil, for you are with me; your rod and your staff, they comfort me. You prepare a table before me in the presence of my enemies. You anoint my head with oil; my cup overflows. Surely your goodness and love will follow me all the days of my life, and I will dwell in the house of the Lord forever."

Psalm 23

PRAYER REQUESTS

Record things you and your children would like to pray over here. Be sure to check back and praise the Lord when He answers. Prompt your kids to think about praying for others. Read Matthew 6:9-13 for how Jesus taught us to pray. As you study the Word notice the pattern of Biblical prayers and prayer requests and try to learn from the Word.

_____   _____

_____   _____

_____   _____

_____   _____

_____   _____

WEEK 1, DAY 1

♪ Lover of My Soul- Kari Jobe

Read to student:

Welcome to unit 5 of our school year! In this unit, we will be studying Europe, birds, and fish, finishing the book of Luke, and starting the book of Acts. Are you ready for more learning?! Have you heard of a man named Zacchaeus in the Bible? There is a fun song about him. We remember that he was short, but it is also good to remember that in addition to being short Zacchaeus was a tax collector. Tax collectors took the people's money to give to the Romans. They were not well-liked and they often took more money than they had to so they could become wealthy. It is understandable that the people did not understand why Jesus chose to go to Zacchaeus' house. Jesus looks at the heart of people and knows who is ready to repent and turn towards obeying God!

 Please pray with your kids. Encourage them to pray also.

▶ Watch "Zacchaeus" from Cedarmont Kids on YouTube
*If you know the motions encourage your kids to do them too!

Scripture Memory Psalm 23

✓ While you read the Bible have your kids color their sheet in their workbook.

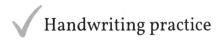 Bible Reading: Luke 19

Have the student(s) tell back what you read. Offer help along the way and kindly explain what you expect when they tell back a story. Be encouraging and compliment.

✓ Handwriting practice

Review

- Say the ABCs
- (1st +) What are nouns and verbs? (Noun- person, place, or thing. Verb- a word that shows action.)
- (1st +) When do we capitalize the first letter of a word? (Beginning of a sentence, proper noun, and the pronoun I.)
- We are going to learn (practice) the calendar. Do you know how many days are in a week? How many months are in a year?
  Say the days of the week and the months of the year.

 Language Arts Section in Student Workbook

 Do you remember when we painted story rocks? We are going to read about Jesus' death, burial, and resurrection this week. Today we are going to paint another set of story rocks to help us tell this most important event!

Story Rocks:
- Flat rocks to paint
- Paint suitable for rock painting
- Paintbrush
- Recommended rocks: praying hands, Jesus, a crown of thorns, cross, grave, angel, empty tomb, disciples (+ others)

Read out loud to your children. This is a great time to read historical books. Be sure to choose books that are written from a Christian perspective or audit them closely for anything that isn't God-glorifying and true. Children grades 1-5 should also spend time reading age-appropriate books.

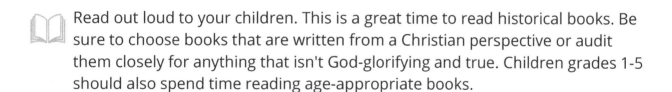

CHECK LIST

- ☐ Worship
- ☐ Bible Reading
- ☐ Art Project

- ☐ Individual reading/reading out loud
- ☐ Complete worksheets with each child
- ☐ Math of choice

WEEK 1, DAY 2

He Reigns- Newsboys

*Please get a coin for each child before today's lesson

Read to student:

I am going to give you a coin to look at. Can you tell me whose image is on this coin? (Help with the answer, explain that former Presidents are on US money.)
It was the same in Jesus' day. The image of a man named Caesar was on the coins. Caesar was the ruler of the Roman world. Jesus gave a wise answer when He was asked about paying taxes. Although some people spied on Jesus and tried to trap Him, He was thoughtful with His answers. Try as they may, the people eventually had to use dishonest witnesses when they brought Jesus to trial.

Jesus told the people to give Caesar what was Ceasar's and to give to God what was God's. What do you think He meant by this?

 Please pray with your kids. Encourage them to pray also.

Scripture Memory Psalm 23

 While you read the Bible have your kids color their sheet in their workbook.

Bible Reading: Luke 20-21

Have the student(s) tell back what you read. Offer help along the way and kindly explain what you expect when they tell back a story. Be encouraging and compliment them.

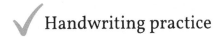 Handwriting practice

Practical Learning   Have students repeat these facts after you.

- There are 24 hours in a day, 60 minutes in an hour, and 60 seconds in a minute.
- There are 52 weeks in a year and 7 days in a week,.
- "Thirty days hath September, April, June, and November; all the rest have 31 except February which has 28, except on leap year when it has 29."
- There are 365 days in a year, leap year has 366.

✓ Language Arts Section in Student Workbook

Look at a globe or map with your child(ren), and show them Europe. Point out different countries and ask them to begin thinking about which country they would like to study.

Read to student:

Today we are going to begin learning about Europe. There are 44 countries in Europe and a population of over 746 million. English and French are the most common language, however, there are over 24 official languages. Europe has many incredible historical sites that people enjoy visiting.

Read a continent book about Europe

✓ Continent Study in Student Workbook

Read out loud to your children, this is a great time to read historical books. Be sure to choose books that are written from a Christian perspective or audit them closely for anything that isn't God-glorifying and true. Children grades 1-5 should also spend time reading age-appropriate books.

CHECK LIST

- ☐ Worship
- ☐ Bible Reading
- ☐ Complete worksheets with each child
- ☐ Individual reading/reading out loud
- ☐ Math of choice

 WEEK 1, DAY 3

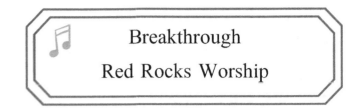
Read to student:

The Last Supper was Jesus' last meal with His disciples before He went to the cross for our sins. Jesus was celebrating the Passover feast. Do you remember when we learned about Passover? The Jewish people had been celebrating Passover and remembering what God had done for them for many years. Jesus was following His Father's commands. Jesus became the ultimate Passover sacrifice when He died on the cross.

Have you taken communion before? It is what we call the elements that Jesus said to remember Him with. The wine represents His blood and the unleavened bread of His body. At this meal, Jesus said He was establishing a New Covenant in His own blood. We are so blessed to have this covenant!

The Bible: the inspired Word of God ▶ Learn the books of the Bible to song

66 books make up one, big book

39 books in the OT, 27 books in the NT

 Please pray with your kids. Encourage them to pray also.

Scripture Memory Psalm 23

 While you read the Bible have your kids color their sheet in their workbook.

Bible Reading: Luke 22

Have the student(s) tell back what you read. Offer help along the way and kindly explain what you expect when they tell back a story. Be encouraging and compliment.

Question: Which disciple betrayed Jesus?

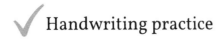 Handwriting practice

💡 Science

On the fifth day of creation, God created fish and birds. Swarms of creatures for the heavens above and the waters. Do you have a favorite kind of bird or fish? Both fish and birds are important food sources for many people. They give us eggs, a protein source, and some people enjoy them as pets. Have you heard the word habitat before? A habitat is the home of a living creature, plant, or organism. We are going to learn about birds, fish, and their habitats during this unit.

FISH BREATHE
SCIENCE ACTIVITY

We will need:
- A coffee filter
- Rubberband or a way to secure the coffee filter
- Water
- 1 TBS of ground coffee
- 2 cups

We are going to do an activity that shows how fish breathe. Fish take in water through their mouths and their gills trap and absorb oxygen. In our activity, the coffee will represent oxygen. We will see what happens to the "oxygen" in water.

- Place the ground coffee in the water
- Place the coffee filter over the second cup and secure
- Pour the coffee water through the filter
- Observe what happens to the water and coffee ground

▶ Watch "Fish | Educational Video for Kids" from Happy Learning English on Youtube.

Science Worksheet

178

Practical Learning

Present these to your family without causing your kids to feel afraid. These are wise things we must teach.

- What do we do in the event of a fire? *Also teach stop, drop, and roll
- What do we do in the event of a natural disaster *fill in with applicable events such as earthquakes, tornadoes, or other.
- Should you ever go with a stranger? NO! Even if they tell you that they know your mom and dad you need to run and immediately come to find one of your parents.

 Language Arts Section in Student Workbook

 ## Observation Walk

Go on a walk outdoors and try to <u>observe</u> in creation what you <u>studied</u> in Science. Allow children to bring a notebook if they want to record their observations.
Use these three points to help start the discussion:

1	2	3
Look	**Factor**	**Observe**
Discuss what you are looking for. Is there a location you could go to observe fish or perhaps their habitat?	Talk about the possibilities of seeing what you studied. Is the water frozen?	Did you find what you were looking for? Why? Why not? Did you learn something from seeing this in creation?

 ### CHECK LIST

- ☐ Worship
- ☐ Bible Reading
- ☐ Complete worksheets with each child
- ☐ Individual reading/reading out loud
- ☐ Math of choice

WEEK 1, DAY 4

Read to student:

Let's play Bible trivia today! I am going to ask questions, and you tell me the right answer as fast as you can. (In our family we offer chocolate chips or other small treats for correct answers. It makes Bible trivia extra sweet and the kids really enjoy it. If you are interested in more questions than are provided download our free Bible trivia printable on www.lampandlightmerchandise.com)

Bible Trivia

1. What day did God create the birds and fish?
2. What did Jesus give as the elements to represent His body and blood?
3. Who climbed a tree to see Jesus?
4. Name one miracle Jesus performed.
5. How many apostles were there?
6. Say one of your memory verses.
7. What was Jesus' first public miracle?
8. How can we be saved?

 Please pray with your kids. Encourage them to pray also.

Scripture Memory Psalm 23

✓ While you read the Bible have your children color the picture on their handwriting sheet. Older children may help with the reading.

 Bible Reading: Luke 23-24

Have the student(s) tell back what you read. Offer help along the way and kindly explain what you expect when they tell back a story. Be encouraging and compliment them.

Question: How does it make you feel to read about Jesus' death, burial, and resurrection?

✓ Handwriting Project   *Third and up write from memory.

At the end of each week have your student practice their best handwriting. Remove this sheet and share with a friend, family member, or persecuted/imprisoned Christian (send through Voice of the Martyrs). Have children 3rd and up address the envelope and write their return address.

Practical Learning

Have students repeat these facts after you. *Give practical examples and hands on demonstrations when possible and when needed.

- Say the Armor of God (Helmet of salvation, the breastplate of righteousness, the belt of truth, feet shod with the readiness of the gospel of peace, shield of faith, sword of the Spirit which is the Word of God.
- Measurement is broken down into units. An inch is a common unit of measurement. There are 12 inches in a foot, and 3 feet in a yard.

✓ Review anything from this week that your children struggled with. (Examples: Sight words, letters)

✓ Language Arts Section in Student Workbook

📖 Read out loud to your children. This is a great time to read historical books. Be sure to choose books that are written from a Christian perspective or audit them closely for anything that isn't God-glorifying and true. Children grades 1-5 should also spend time reading age-appropriate books.

CHECK LIST

- ☐ Worship
- ☐ Bible Reading
- ☐ Complete worksheets with each child
- ☐ Individual reading/reading out loud
- ☐ Math of choice

WEEK 2, DAY 1

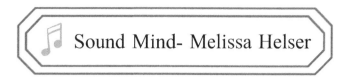
Read to student:

Today we are going to start the book of Acts. Do you remember how we learned that Luke wrote both Luke and Acts? Consider this part two! Part two begins after Jesus was raised from the dead and was the beginning of the gospel being spread into all of the world. Jesus ascended into heaven and is now seated at the right hand of the throne of God. He taught His disciples well so they could in turn teach others. You and I know Jesus because the disciples obeyed what we call The Great Commission. (Read Matthew 28:16-20).

▶ Watch "Overview: Acts 1-7" from The Bible Project on YouTube

🙏 Please pray with your kids. Encourage them to pray also.

Scripture Memory Psalm 23

✓ While you read the Bible have your kids color the picture on their handwriting sheet.

📖 Bible Reading: Acts 1

182

✓ Handwriting practice

✓ Language Arts Section in Student Workbook

Review + Focus

- What continent did we study in our last unit? Tell me one fact about it!
- How would you share the gospel with someone? Start with telling them who Jesus is. (Help as needed. Encourage your kids to use what they practice to really share about Jesus with kids they encounter in your neighborhood, at the park, or otherwise.)
- Tell me one prayer that God has answered for you!
- Tell me one thing you are thankful for!

 Art Project:
We are going to learn to fold paper pouches and envelopes today. After you fold a pouch or envelope please come up with a small treat to share with a neighbor or friend. This could be something like some small candies, a homemade cookie, or a couple of bags of tea. Write a nice note to go with your gift.
Find ideas for how to fold DIY paper pouches on Pinterest at lampandlightliving, Unit 5 board.

Read out loud to your children, this is a great time to read historical books. Be sure to choose books that are written from a Christian perspective or audit them closely for anything that isn't God-glorifying and true. Children grades 1-5 should also spend time reading age-appropriate books.

CHECK LIST

- ☐ Worship
- ☐ Bible Reading
- ☐ Art Project

- ☐ Individual reading/reading out loud
- ☐ Complete worksheets with each child
- ☐ Math of choice

 WEEK 2, DAY 2

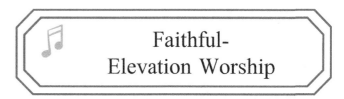
Faithful-
Elevation Worship

Read to student:

Jesus promised His disciples that He would not leave them alone, but that He would send the Holy Spirit. He actually said it was better for them that He would go to the Father and that the Holy Spirit would come. We know by how Jesus spoke that this was a significant event!

The day that the Holy Spirit was poured out is called Pentecost. It was a long-established Biblical feast day. The LORD had told the Israelites to observe this day many, many years before. Jesus' death, burial, and resurrection happened on important days on the Biblical calendar. The prophet Joel prophesied that the Holy Spirit would be poured out on God's people, both male, and female. The Holy Spirit is the Spirit of the one true God. As believers in Jesus, we are able to be filled with the Holy Spirit and He enables us to live powerful and pleasing lives to God's glory.

 Please pray with your kids. Encourage them to pray also.

Scripture Memory Psalm 23

 While you read the Bible have your kids color the picture on their handwriting sheet.

 Bible Reading: Acts 2

Have the student(s) tell back what you read. Offer help along the way and kindly explain what you expect when they tell back a story. Be encouraging and compliment them.

Question:
Where were Jesus' followers gathered when the Holy Spirit was poured out?
What sound did they hear? How did the Holy Spirit appear?

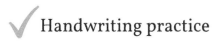 Handwriting practice

Practical Learning Have students repeat these facts after you.

- A penny is worth 1 cent, a nickel is worth 5 cents, a dime is worth 10 cents, a quarter is worth 25 cents.
- There are 100 cents in a dollar.
- For older kids challenge them to tell you what amount of money different combinations of coins makes.

 Language Arts Section in Student Workbook

 Read to student:

Do you remember what you learned last week about Europe? Today we are going to have some fun with what we learned! We are going to make the information you learned into a visual report that you can share with others. There is a sheet in your workbook to help you get started.

Things to consider encouraging your child to add:
- Visual appeal with colors, themes, and facts
- Stickers, printed or magazine images, or drawings
- Number of countries
- Top natural resources
- Main religion, percent of known Christians *Be sure to share that this isn't always accurate if a country has laws against Christianity. We could have brothers and sisters in Christ not openly declaring their religion.
- Main bodies of water
- Any significant landmarks- both natural and man-made

Read out loud to your children. This is a great time to read historical books. Be sure to choose books that are written from a Christian perspective or audit them closely for anything that isn't God-glorifying and true. Children grades 1-5 should also spend time reading age-appropriate books.

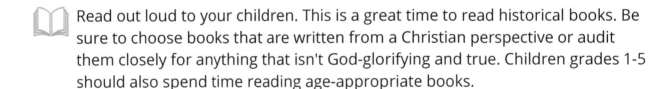

CHECK LIST

- ☐ Worship
- ☐ Bible Reading
- ☐ Complete worksheets with each child
- ☐ Individual reading/reading out loud
- ☐ Math of choice

 WEEK 2, DAY 3

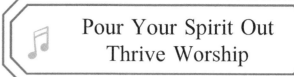
Pour Your Spirit Out
Thrive Worship

Read to student:

Do you remember Peter's response when he was asked if he knew Jesus, as Jesus was being tried before dying on the cross?

Yes, Peter denied Jesus. In His mercy, Jesus restored Peter (John 21:15-19). He forgave him and told him to strengthen his brothers. Peter went from denying Jesus to boldly proclaiming Him after being filled with the Holy Spirit. What a change! As we read today, notice when the Bible says Peter was filled with the Holy Spirit when he spoke.

Being filled with the Holy Spirit brings boldness and the ability to clearly speak the gospel- the good news about Jesus- and the word of God.

Today we will read what was the beginning of the Church as we know it. The Church isn't a place, it is God's people gathered together. Everyone who believed in Jesus was one in heart and mind. They shared what they had with each other.

 Please pray with your kids. Encourage them to pray also.

Scripture Memory Psalm 23

 While you read the Bible have your kids color the picture on their handwriting sheet.

 Bible Reading: Acts 3-4

Have the student(s) tell back what you read. Offer help along the way and kindly explain what you expect when they tell back a story. Be encouraging and compliment them.

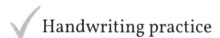 Handwriting practice

Science

Last week we learned about fish. This week you are going to choose one species of fish to study. We are going to do research to understand the particulars of the fish you choose. We will learn if this fish is a freshwater or saltwater fish, its habitat, what it eats, where it thrives, if it migrates, and much more!

Instead of doing an experiment, we will work on making a mini presentation about the fish you choose.

Practical Learning Present these to your family without causing your kids to feel afraid. These are wise things we must teach.

- What do we do in the event of a fire? *Also teach stop, drop, and roll
- What do we do in the event of a natural disaster *Fill in with applicable events such as earthquakes, tornadoes, or other.
- Should you ever go with a stranger? NO! Even if they tell you that they know your mom and dad you need to run and immediately come to find one of your parents.

 Language Arts Section in Student Workbook

 Observation Walk

Go on a walk outdoors and try to <u>observe</u> in creation what you <u>studied</u> in Science. Allow children to bring a notebook if they want to record their observations.
Use these three points to help start the discussion:

Look

Discuss what you are looking for. Find the location around your outdoor environment with the highest probability.

Factor

Talk about the possibilities of seeing what you studied. Is there a place nearby where you can see fish? What about the species you chose?

Observe

Did you find what you were looking for? Why? Why not? Did you learn something from seeing this in creation?

CHECK LIST

- ☐ Worship
- ☐ Bible Reading
- ☐ Complete worksheets with each child
- ☐ Individual reading/reading out loud
- ☐ Math of choice

WEEK 2, DAY 4

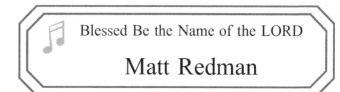
Read to student:

Have you ever lied? Did you get caught? Today we are going to read a very serious story of a couple who tried to lie to the Holy Spirit. God takes what we say seriously. We cannot say we did something that we didn't really do. God knows the motives of our hearts and the truth. Even if it seems you get away with telling a lie it is important to know that even if a human does not know, God always does. More than anything we should want to please God. God gives us parents and teachers to help us learn, but ultimately we answer to God. Someday when we stand before God we can't say that our parents served God. That won't be enough. Each of us must choose to love and obey Jesus on our own. God's grace is sufficient for you and it is sufficient for me. I am so thankful for salvation through Jesus!

 Please pray with your kids. Encourage them to pray also.

Scripture Memory Psalm 23

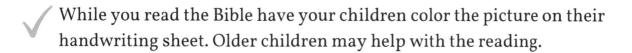 While you read the Bible have your children color the picture on their handwriting sheet. Older children may help with the reading.

📖 Bible Reading: Acts 5

Have the student(s) tell back what you read. Offer help along the way and kindly explain what you expect when they tell back a story. Be encouraging and compliment them.

✓ Handwriting Project   *Third and up write from memory.

At the end of each week have your student practice their best handwriting. Remove this sheet and share with a friend, family member, or persecuted/imprisoned Christian (send through Voice of the Martyrs). Have children 3rd and up address the envelope and write their return address.

Practical Learning

Have students repeat these facts after you. *Give practical examples and hands on demonstrations when possible and when needed.

- Say the fruits of the Spirit: love, joy, peace, patience, kindness, goodness, faithfulness, gentleness, and self-control.
- Weight is how we know how heavy something is. An ounce is a small unit of weight. There are 16 ounces in a pound.

Read to student:

Give time for them to answer questions and remind them when needed.

Let's review what we have learned this week.
Can you tell me something we learned from the Bible?
Tell me one fact about Europe?

✓ Review anything from this week that your children struggled with. (Examples: sight words, letters)

✓ Language Arts Section in Student Workbook

📖 Read out loud to your children. This is a great time to read historical books. Be sure to choose books that are written from a Christian perspective or audit them closely for anything that isn't God-glorifying and true. Children grades 1-5 should also spend time reading age appropriate books.

✓ Help your child with their worksheet and report about a historical figure.

If you have not completed a book about a historical figure, do your best to help your child find a historical person of interest to use for this exercise. Add words your child may struggle with when writing to next week's spelling list.

CHECK LIST

- ☐ Worship
- ☐ Bible Reading
- ☐ Complete worksheets with each child
- ☐ Individual reading/reading out loud
- ☐ Math of choice

WEEK 3, DAY 1

Read to student:

Stephen is a special man we learn about in the Bible. He was the first martyr. A martyr is someone who is willing to die for Jesus' name. We are going to read about Stephen today. Notice how God is with him the entire time and how God enables Stephen to speak boldly even when people did not like what he was saying.

We know that this earth is not our home. We have heaven to look forward to. The Bible says that even if our earthly bodies are destroyed we have a better future to look forward to with Jesus. When people who are believers in Jesus die we do not have to grieve in the same way the world grieves. We can be sad because we will miss them, but we know we will see them when we spend eternity with Jesus! Jesus promised that He is going to prepare a place for us and that He will take us there to be with Him. We have hope for the future. We can trust Jesus!

 Please pray with your kids. Encourage them to pray also.

Scripture Memory Psalm 23   Found at the beginning of this unit.

 While you read the Bible have your kids color the picture on their handwriting sheet.

 Bible Reading: Acts 6-7

Have the student(s) act out the story or a portion of the story that you read. Offer help with ideas and narration. You can make this as simple or complex as you wish.

✓ Handwriting practice

✓ Language Arts Section in Student Workbook

Review

- How many days did it take God to create the world?
- Tell me the continents we have studied so far.
- Do you remember your memory verse from last week?
- Tell me one thing you are thankful for!

 Later this week we are going to read in the Bible about a woman named Dorcas/Tabbitha. She used her skill of sewing to bless others. I want you to brainstorm and think of something you know how to make that you can use to bless another believer. If you are able to sew you can make a clothing item just like Dorcas/Tabitha. Here are a few other ideas:

- Make a spice blend to gift
- Carve or craft something to gift
- Crochet or knit a clothing item
- Cook a meal to share with someone who is sick or in need

Read out loud to your children. This is a great time to read historical books. Be sure to choose books that are written from a Christian perspective or audit them closely for anything that isn't God-glorifying and true. Children grades 1-5 should also spend time reading age-appropriate books.

CHECK LIST

☐ Worship

☐ Bible Reading

☐ Art Project

☐ Individual reading/reading out loud

☐ Complete worksheets with each child

☐ Math of choice

WEEK 3, DAY 2

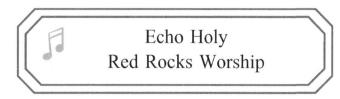

Echo Holy
Red Rocks Worship

Read to student:

It is hard for us to imagine being persecuted for simply believing in Jesus. We have learned a bit about persecution already this year. In some countries believing in Jesus is enough to get a person excommunicated from their family, kicked out of their town, fired from their job, and maybe even killed. Persecution is not new. It began with Jesus and His early followers. Do you know what is neat about persecution? Although it is something that is meant for evil, God uses it for good! Many times it is the way the gospel spreads! That is what happened with the early church and it still happens today. When people who believe in Jesus are persecuted occasionally they move, and when they do they take the good news about Jesus with them!

There is one other thing I want to point out to you that we are going to read about today. Do you remember how Jesus' followers received the gift of the Holy Spirit? Today I want you to notice how those who believed in Jesus in Samaria received the Holy Spirit!

Today when we pray let's pray specifically for our brothers and sisters in Christ who are persecuted for Jesus' name.

 Please pray with your kids. Encourage them to pray also.

Scripture Memory Psalm 23

 While you read the Bible have your kids color the picture on their handwriting sheet.

 Bible Reading: Acts 8

Have the student(s) tell back what you read. Offer help along the way and kindly explain what you expect when they tell back a story. Be encouraging and compliment.

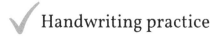 Handwriting practice

Practical Learning   Have students repeat these facts after you.

- Freezing temperature of water is 32 degrees F.
- Boiling temperature of water is 212 degrees F.
- Water expands when it freezes.
- Water can be in different forms. It can be a liquid, a solid (ice), and a gas (steam).

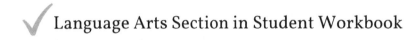 Language Arts Section in Student Workbook

 Read to student:

Today we are going to study one country in Europe. If you have not already done so, please choose a country to study. We are going to work together to find the answers to the questions on your worksheet. Next week we will choose a project to do for the country you chose. You will have different options to choose from. You may look ahead in your book now and decide which project you will do. While we study, we will look for information to prepare for next week.

Every country is unique. They have distinct features both geographically and culturally. Some countries are very diverse. Take the United States for example.- There are different areas of the United States that have very different cultures. How we talk even sounds a little bit different! Certain areas have unique styles of food that vary, the climate varies, and the natural resources and job opportunities vary. While there is variation within a country, a country shares a common government, currency (money), main language, and laws.

Read out loud to your children. This is a great time to read historical books. Be sure to choose books that are written from a Christian perspective or audit them closely for anything that isn't God-glorifying and true. Children grades 1-5 should also spend time reading age-appropriate books.

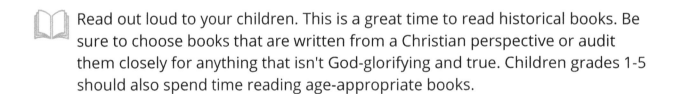 CHECK LIST

- ☐ Worship
- ☐ Bible Reading
- ☐ Complete worksheets with each child
- ☐ Individual reading/reading out loud
- ☐ Math of choice

WEEK 3, DAY 3

Throne Room
Kim Walker-Smith

Read to student:

Think about the brightest light you have ever seen. Did you still have vision after you looked at it? Imagine what light from heaven might look like!

Today we are going to learn about Saul/Paul! Paul is the author of much of the New Testament and definitely one of the most influential people we learn about in Scripture. Do you know that he started off as a bad guy? He approved of the stoning of Stephen and he was eager to persecute the Church! Of course, he thought he was doing the right thing. He was Jewish and he did not believe that Jesus was the Messiah so he truly thought he was offering a service to God. Thankfully, God intervened. I want you to always remember that. God has the power to take bad guys and turn them into Christians who love Jesus! There is no one who is too far gone. No one who is too "bad". Jesus saves sinners. All of us.

One common misconception about Paul is that Jesus changed his name. Scripture does not say that. It is likely that Paul was simply the Greek version of Saul.

 Please pray with your kids. Encourage them to pray also.

Scripture Memory Psalm 23

 While you read the Bible have your kids color the picture on their handwriting sheet.

 Bible Reading: Acts 9

Have the student(s) tell back what you read. Offer help along the way and kindly explain what you expect when they tell back a story. Be encouraging and compliment them.

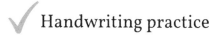 Handwriting practice

☀️ Science

What else did God create on day five of creation? That's right! Birds! Today we are going to study birds. Tell me one thing you already know about birds.

Birds are fascinating. There are many types of birds who live in a wide variety of climates. Did you know some birds migrate? Some birds fly many miles multiple times a year to find the right climate and food sources.

▶️ Watch "All About Birds" from Free School on Youtube.

✓ Science Activity and Worksheet

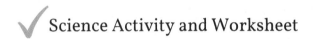

BIRDS IN A "V"
SCIENCE ACTIVITY

You will need:

- A fan
- A strip of paper
- Pencil (optional: draw birds on the paper)

Directions:
Why do birds fly in a "V"? We are going to conduct an experiment to find out!

*Note: Be sure to supervise carefully while near a fan.
To begin, we are going to start with our strip of paper flat.
Try to hold the paper up to the fan. Is it easy?
Now, fold the paper into a "V" and try again.
Is it easier to hold?

Birds may fly in a "V" because it makes flying easier as there is a reduction in wind resistance. Fun fact: Squadrons of planes can save fuel by flying this way!

Practical Learning

- Each of the 50 states has a capital city. The capital of our state_____
- Washington D.C. is the capital of the United States.
- There are 12 tribes of Israel.
- Jesus had 12 disciples.

 Language Arts Section in Student Workbook

 Observation Walk

Go on a walk outdoors and try to <u>observe</u> in creation what you <u>studied</u> in Science. Allow children to bring a notebook if they want to record their observations.
Use these three points to help start the discussion:

1

Look

Discuss what you are looking for.
Find the location around your outdoor environment with the highest probability.

2

Factor

Talk about the possibilities of seeing what you studied. What birds are in your area? Can you spot any nests?

3

Observe

Did you find what you were looking for?
Why? Why not?
Did you learn something from seeing this in creation?

CHECK LIST

- ☐ Worship
- ☐ Bible Reading
- ☐ Complete worksheets with each child
- ☐ Individual reading/reading out loud
- ☐ Math of choice

 WEEK 3, DAY 4

He Reigns
Newsboys

Read to student:

Do you understand the difference between a Jew and a Gentile? We are going to review this because it is important to understand how the Gospel spread throughout the world!

A Jew is a person who is a descendant from the tribe of Judah or Benjamin, but it is also a religion. It is possible that anyone who maintained their identity as an Israelite was considered Jewish by the time the New Testament was written. (Consider that Joseph, Zechariah, Elizabeth, and Anna were all from other tribes). A person could also become Jewish by totally changing their lifestyle and giving up their background. There was always a provision for foreigners to join God's people. (Consider the mixed multitude that left Egypt, Rahab, and Ruth.)

A Gentile is essentially anyone who is not Jewish by birth or religion. Some Gentiles worshipped God, many did not. However, they were always separate from God's chosen people. In Acts 10, which we will read today, things dramatically changed! Listen to God's thoughts about the Gentiles He wanted to save. The Good News truly is for everyone of every tribe, tongue, and nation!

 Please pray with your kids. Encourage them to pray also.

Scripture Memory Psalm 23

 While you read the Bible have your children color the picture on their handwriting sheet. Older children may help with the reading.

Bible Reading: Acts 10

Have the student(s) tell back what you read. Offer help along the way and kindly explain what you expect when they tell back a story. Be encouraging and compliment them.

Handwriting Project   *Third and up write from memory.

At the end of each week have your student practice their best handwriting. Remove this sheet and share with a friend, family member, or persecuted/imprisoned Christian (send through Voice of the Martyrs). Have children 3rd and up address the envelope and write their return address.

197

Practical Learning

Have students repeat these facts after you. *Give practical examples and hands-on demonstrations when possible and when needed.

- Say the Lord's Prayer.
- Volume is another way we know how much of something there is, or how much is needed. We use these often in recipes. There are 8 ounces in one cup, 2 cups in a pint, 2 pints in a quart, and 4 quarts in a gallon.

Read to student:

Give time for them to answer questions and remind them when needed.

Let's review what we have learned this week.

Can you tell me something we learned from the Bible?

Tell me one fact about fish or birds that you have learned.

✓ Review anything from this week that your children struggled with. (Examples: sight words, letters)

✓ Language Arts Section in Student Workbook

📖 Read out loud to your children. This is a great time to read historical books. Be sure to choose books that are written from a Christian perspective or audit them closely for anything that isn't God-glorifying and true.

✓ Spend a few minutes with each child checking in on their reading progress. Make sure older children are able to decode words in syllables. Make sure younger children are recognizing their sight words within the text of a book.

CHECK LIST

- ☐ Worship
- ☐ Bible Reading
- ☐ Complete worksheets with each child
- ☐ Individual reading/reading out loud
- ☐ Math of choice

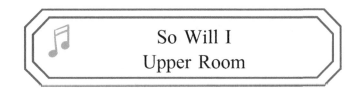
So Will I
Upper Room

Read to student:

I am SO thankful that salvation through Jesus is for everyone! Last week we read about Peter receiving a vision from the Lord to tell him that Gentiles were clean and acceptable to God. Today we will read about Peter explaining that to others and about his miraculous escape from prison!

Have you ever been so excited about something that you didn't know what to do?

When Peter was led out of prison by an angel, the servant girl who answered the door to the home he went to was so filled with joy that she didn't even open the door for Peter!

Try to imagine what that would have been like. Think about being gathered with other believers and praying and praying for a person. What would you do if God did such an amazing miracle? God still does miracles. When we pray we can believe that He will answer according to His will!

 Please pray with your kids. Encourage them to pray also.

Scripture Memory Psalm 23

✓ While you read the Bible have your kids color the picture on their handwriting sheet.

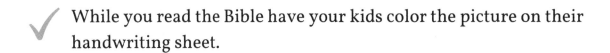 Bible Reading: Acts 11-12

Have the student(s) act out the story or a portion of the story that you read. Offer help with ideas and narration. You can make this as simple or complex as you wish.

✓ Handwriting practice

✓ Language Arts Section in Student Workbook

Review

- Tell me one of the 10 Commandments.
- Do you remember your memory verse from last week?
- Tell me one thing you are thankful for!

 One thing that is very special about the Church is our love for one another. Jesus said that the world would see Him when they see our love for each other. Paul and the other Church leaders wrote many letters to the churches in various cities. We have read some of those letters this year. Often times these letters included encouragement and instruction.

For our art project this week we are going to make a special card to send to a brother or sister in Christ. Choose an encouraging Bible verse from one of the New Testament letters to include with your card.

- Print, stamp, or use stickers to create a card
- Check lampandlightliving Unit 5 Pinterest board for inspiring ideas
- Use Canva to create a printed card
- Help your child choose a verse to write and assist them if needed. This is also a great time for older children to practice addressing an envelope. Don't forget to teach proper stamp placement and remember that bulky cards may require additional postage.

 Read out loud to your children. This is a great time to read historical books. Be sure to choose books that are written from a Christian perspective or audit them closely for anything that isn't God-glorifying and true. Children grades 1-5 should also spend time reading age-appropriate books.

CHECK LIST

- [ ] Worship
- [ ] Bible Reading
- [ ] Art Project

- [ ] Individual reading/reading out loud
- [ ] Complete worksheets with each child
- [ ] Math of choice

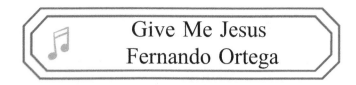
♫ Give Me Jesus
Fernando Ortega

Read to student:

The Holy Spirit is vital to our lives as followers of Jesus.

Today when we read in Acts pay attention to how the Holy Spirit speaks and sends people. We can live our lives directed by the very Spirit of God! Taking time to listen to the Lord is important. We know that God cannot lie. The Holy Spirit will always lead us into greater obedience to the Word of God because He is God. The Holy Spirit comforts us, convicts us, and speaks to us.

Notice how Paul is guided by the Holy Spirit and his reverence for God's Word and the story of Scripture. Notice how he speaks to the people at the synagogue.

The synagogue was a gathering place that Jewish people met on Sabbath days to worship God and read Scripture. Jesus also went to the synagogue. We see members of the Church gather there, but they also gathered in homes. Listen carefully when I read, and you will hear that there were also God-fearing Gentiles gathered at the synagogue.

 Please pray with your kids. Encourage them to pray also.

Scripture Memory Psalm 23

✓ While you read the Bible have your kids color the picture on their handwriting sheet.

 Bible Reading: Acts 13

Have the student(s) tell back what you read. Offer help along the way and kindly explain what you expect when they tell back a story. Be encouraging and compliment them.

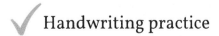 Handwriting practice

Practical Learning Have students repeat these facts after you.

- There are 5,280 feet in a mile.
- What did Jesus say the greatest commandments are? (Matt.
  1. Love the LORD your God with all your heart, soul, and strength
  2. The second is like it, love your neighbor as yourself.
     All of the Law and prophets hang on these two commands.

✓ Language Arts Section in Student Workbook

 Read to student:

Today we get to do our country project! Are you excited? Can you tell me why you chose the option you chose for our project? What is something that drew you to this country? Let's pray specifically for this country:
1. Pray for believers there to live for the Lord, love His Word, share the gospel, and seek first the kingdom of God.
2. Pray for their government officials to come to know Jesus and to have the wisdom to wisely lead their people. Pray for freedom to worship Jesus and peace.
3. Pray for missionaries in this country and leaders of God's people. Pray for safety and that they would not grow weary in doing good.
4. Pray for the Lord to send more gospel workers into the harvest. Jesus said the harvest is plentiful but the laborers few! (Matthew 9:35-38)

Note: Don't forget to have them present their project to a family member or friend.

✓ Geography Section in Student Workbook

 Read out loud to your children. This is a great time to read historical books. Be sure to choose books that are written from a Christian perspective or audit them closely for anything that isn't God-glorifying and true. Children grades 1-5 should also spend time reading age-appropriate books.

CHECK LIST

- ☐ Worship
- ☐ Bible Reading
- ☐ Complete worksheets with each child
- ☐ Individual reading/reading out loud
- ☐ Math of choice

WEEK 4, DAY 3

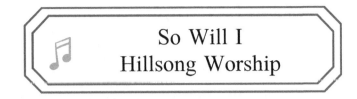
♪ So Will I
Hillsong Worship

Read to student:

Do you know anyone who is sick or has physical trouble? How about anyone who can't walk? Today we are going to read about a man who couldn't walk. He could not walk for his entire life until the Lord healed him. Wouldn't that be amazing to see?!

The people of his town sure thought so. They started to treat Paul and Barnabas like they were gods. Paul and Barnabas were quick to stop them and gave credit to the living God who created the heavens and the earth.

Paul and Barnabas told many people about Jesus, and many believed and became disciples! Paul and Barnabas also encouraged and strengthened the disciples. They appointed elders in each Church and committed them to the Lord.

▶ Watch "Overview: Acts 13-28" from The Bible Project on Youtube.

 Please pray with your kids. Encourage them to pray also.

Scripture Memory Psalm 23

✓ While you read the Bible have your kids color the picture on their handwriting sheet.

📖 Bible Reading: Acts 14-15

Have the student(s) tell back what you read. Offer help along the way and kindly explain what you expect when they tell back a story. Be encouraging and compliment them.

✓ Language Arts Section in Student Workbook

💡 Science

Last week we learned about birds. This week you are going to choose one species to study. We are going to do research to understand the particulars of the bird you choose. Instead of doing an experiment, we will work on making a mini presentation about the bird you choose.

Practical Learning

- Say the books of the Bible either from memory or with song.
- For students that are confident readers, have them do a couple of Sword Drills. Sword Drills are fun competitions to see how fast you can find something in the Bible. Acts 14:21, Psalm 91:1

 Language Arts Section in Student Workbook

 Observation Walk

Go on a walk outdoors and try to <u>observe</u> in creation what you <u>studied</u> in Science. Allow children to bring a notebook if they want to record their observations.
Use these three points to help start the discussion:

Look

Discuss what you
are looking for.
Do you see any birds?
If so, what kinds?

Factor

Talk about the
possibilities of seeing
what you studied.

Observe

Did you find what you
were looking for?
Why? Why not?
Did you learn
something from
seeing this in creation?

CHECK LIST

- ☐ Worship
- ☐ Bible Reading
- ☐ Complete worksheets with each child
- ☐ Individual reading/reading out loud
- ☐ Math of choice

WEEK 4, DAY 4

Read to student:

Acts is an action-packed story, isn't it? Today's reading is no different! There are two special people that we meet briefly in this chapter.

The first is Timothy. Timothy was a companion of Paul. His mother was Jewish and a believer, but it does not seem his father was. He was a Greek and no mention is made of him believing. In Paul's letters to Timothy, he mentions Timothy's mom and grandma's faith. Timothy is encouraging because he was faithful to the Lord, yet only had one parent who was a believer.

The second person we are going to highlight today is Lydia. She was a worshipper of God, she was employed selling purple cloth, she had a family, and the Lord opened her heart to receive the truth about Jesus. She persuaded Paul and his friends to come to her house and she was still willing to receive them in her home even after they were in prison.

There is much we can learn from people in the Bible. Even if we aren't given many details, we can learn from what we are given!

 Please pray with your kids. Encourage them to pray also.

Scripture Memory Psalm 23

✓ While you read the Bible have your children color the picture on their handwriting sheet. Older children may help with the reading.

 Bible Reading: Acts 16

Have the student(s) tell back what you read. Offer help along the way and kindly explain what you expect when they tell back a story. Be encouraging and compliment them.

 Handwriting Project   *Third and up write from memory.

At the end of each week have your student practice their best handwriting. Remove this sheet and share with a friend, family member, or persecuted/imprisoned Christian (send through Voice of the Martyrs). Have children 3rd and up address the envelope and write their return address.

End of unit review:

Give time for them to answer questions and remind them when needed.

Wow! Great job this week! I am enjoying teaching you and learning with you. Let's do a review of some of the things are have learned through this unit!

Can you tell me something we learned from the Bible?

Is there one verse or lesson that really helped you?
Did the LORD comfort or convict you in any area?

What is something you learned about birds and fish?

Tell me a historical person you most enjoyed learning about. Why did you enjoy their story?

What was your favorite thing you learned about Europe?

✓ Review anything from this week that your children struggled with. (Examples: sight words, letters)

✓ Language Arts Section in Student Workbook

📖 Read out loud to your children. This is a great time to read historical books. Be sure to choose books that are written from a Christian perspective or audit them closely for anything that isn't God-glorifying and true.

✓ Spend a few minutes with each child checking in on their reading progress. Make sure older children are able to decode words into syllables. Make sure younger children are recognizing their sight words within the text of a book.

CHECK LIST

☐ Worship   ☐ Individual reading/reading out loud

☐ Bible Reading   ☐ Math of choice

☐ Complete worksheets with each child

Mini-Unit Study Plan

✓ Choose a topic

✓ Find needed resources- videos, websites, books

✓ Choose activities: field trip, experiment, movie

✓ Find Scriptures that many apply

1

Plan

Work with your child(ren) to come up with the best study for your family. Make a plan and allow them to be involved in finding resources and ideas.

2

Learn

Choose ways that learning will be involved. Examples include a write up, making lists, books to read, and more

3

Enjoy

Have fun! Allow your child to talk to others about their experience. Try to enjoy this week together and foster a desire to learn more.

 WEEK 5 DAILY CHECK LIST

☐ Unit Study   ☐ Math of choice

☐ Unit Study   ☐ Math of choice

☐ Unit Study   ☐ Math of choice

☐ Unit Study   ☐ Math of choice

UNIT Six

GOSPEL FOCUS & EYES ON JESUS

This is our last unit! Congratulations on your diligent and intentional training of your children. Remember to live for the Lord's, "Well done good and faithful servant." No level of education will ever matter or be of any value if our children are not following Jesus. Prioritize time with God and intimacy with the Lord. Don't allow the standards of the world and the hustle and bustle to kill off the good seeds sown. Allow the Holy Spirit to convict both you and your children. Remember, you will not always be there to correct and guide your children so they must be filled with the Holy Spirit so that He can bring comfort and correction to them.

PRAY

Pause and intentionally pray over your school time. Ask the Lord to work through the time you spend educating your children to give you and your children a kingdom-first perspective. Ask the Lord to help you keep your eyes on Jesus. Seek the Lord for opportunities and ways you and your children can share the gospel and pray for anyone you have shared the gospel with. Pray for each of your children that they will know and serve the Lord.

QUESTIONS

1. Am I being intentional with our homeschool time?
2. Are we simply checking boxes or are my children learning to love Jesus and others through our schooling?
3. Do I feel burned out? If so, seek the Lord for new strength
4. How can I best use the time I have with my children? Are we too busy to focus on what matters most?
5. Have I let distractions creep into our day that we need to reduce?

EXTRA
Resources

UNIT VERSE

""The God who made the world and everything in it is the Lord of heaven and earth and does not live in temples built by human hands. And he is not served by human hands, as if he needed anything. Rather, he himself gives everyone life and breath and everything else. From one man he made all the nations, that they should inhabit the whole earth; and he marked out their appointed times in history and the boundaries of their lands. God did this so that they would seek him and perhaps reach out for him and find him, though he is not far from any one of us. 'For in him we live and move and have our being.' As some of your own poets have said, 'We are his offspring.'

"Therefore since we are God's offspring, we should not think that the divine being is like gold or silver or stone—an image made by human design and skill. In the past God overlooked such ignorance, but now he commands all people everywhere to repent. For he has set a day when he will judge the world with justice by the man he has appointed. He has given proof of this to everyone by raising him from the dead."

Acts 17:24-31 *You may wish to shorten this for grades K-2

PRAYER REQUESTS

Record things you and your children would like to pray over here. Be sure to check back and praise the Lord when He answers. Prompt your kids to think about praying for others. Read Matthew 6:9-13 for how Jesus taught us to pray. As you study the Word notice the pattern of Biblical prayers and prayer requests and try to learn from the Word.

_____   _____

_____   _____

_____   _____

 WEEK 1, DAY 1

 ♪ Lover of My Soul- Kari Jobe

Read to student:

Wow! Today we are starting our final unit of the school year! Are you excited? You have learned so much this year and we are going to finish out the year by learning some very important things. We are going to pack a whole lot of learning into this final unit. Are you ready for that? In this unit, we will be studying North and South America, animals, and humans, and finishing out the book of Acts. I am excited to teach you about these topics. I am very happy that you have worked so hard this year on your studies. It is pleasing to God when we are diligent and do our best without grumbling and complaining. What you learn now will be a very important foundation for the rest of your life. Let's get started!

(NOTE: If your school year runs for longer than 30 weeks this is a great unit to spend a bit more time on. North and South America can be split into two unique studies as can humans and animals. Plan to spend more time on each with the resources provided as an outline if possible. If you intend to finish the school year in 30 weeks consider this an introduction to these topics and plan to spend more time on them for next school year.)

 Please pray with your kids. Encourage them to pray also.

 Scripture Memory Acts 17:24-31

✓ While you read the Bible have your kids color their sheet in their workbook.

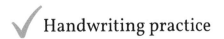 Bible Reading: Acts 17

Have the student(s) tell back what you read. Offer help along the way and kindly explain what you expect when they tell back a story. Be encouraging and compliment them.

✓ Handwriting practice

Review

- Say the ABCs
- (1st +) What are nouns and verbs? (Noun- person, place, or thing. Verb- a word that shows action.)
- (1st +) When do we capitalize the first letter of a word? (Beginning of a sentence, proper noun, and the pronoun I.)
- We are going to learn (practice) the calendar. Do you know how many days are in a week? How many months are in a year?
  Say the days of the week and the months of the year.

 Language Arts Section in Student Workbook

 Today when we read the Bible we read that those who lived in Berea were noble. They received the message about Jesus with eagerness and they examined the Scriptures to see if it was true. At this time the Scriptures were just the Old Testament. The Old Testament proves Jesus is the Messiah through prophecy. Because the Bereans were diligent in their study many of them believed. I want you to learn to be diligent in studying God's Word! Today we are going to assemble a Bible study kit.
*NOTE TO PARENTS: This can be as elaborate as you choose. It can include a significant project like making a Bible case or a gathering of supplies like highlighters, a Bible, and some sticky notes. For younger children encourage them to make drawings on stick notes to include in their Bible when they read. For older children encourage them to take notes and learn to study.

 Read out loud to your children. This is a great time to read historical books. Be sure to choose books that are written from a Christian perspective or audit them closely for anything that isn't God-glorifying and true. Children grades 1-5 should also spend time reading age-appropriate books.

CHECK LIST

- ☐ Worship
- ☐ Bible Reading
- ☐ Art Project

- ☐ Individual reading/reading out loud
- ☐ Complete worksheets with each child
- ☐ Math of choice

 WEEK 1, DAY 2

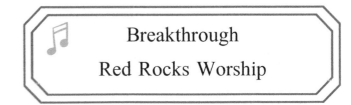

♫ Breakthrough
Red Rocks Worship

Read to student:

Can you imagine being treated badly for sharing about Jesus? Paul was. He was often treated badly. Persecution is what we call being treated badly because of what we believe about Jesus. One night the Lord gave him a very encouraging vision to continue speaking. He told Paul He would be with him and keep him safe. What a blessing and a comfort that must have been to Paul!

In today's reading we will meet Priscilla and Aquila. They are some favorite Bible heroes. They had the Church gather in their home and they worked together as a husband and wife team to advance God's kingdom. The were also tent makers like Paul!

The Bible: the inspired Word of God ▶ Learn the books of the Bible to song
66 books make up one, big book
39 books in the OT, 27 books in the NT

 Please pray with your kids. Encourage them to pray also.

Scripture Memory Acts 17:24-31

✓ While you read the Bible have your kids color their sheet in their workbook.

📖 Bible Reading: Acts 18

Have the student(s) tell back what you read. Offer help along the way and kindly explain what you expect when they tell back a story. Be encouraging and compliment them.

✓ Handwriting practice

Practical Learning   Have students repeat these facts after you.

- There are 24 hours in a day, 60 minutes in an hour, and 60 seconds in a minute.
- There are 52 weeks in a year and 7 days in a week,.
- "Thirty days hath September, April, June, and November; all the rest have 31 except February which has 28, except on leap year when it has 29."
- There are 365 days in a year, leap year has 366.

 Language Arts Section in Student Workbook

 Look at a globe or map with your child(ren), and show them North & South America. Point out different countries and ask them to begin thinking about which country they would like to study.

Read to student:

Today we are going to begin learning about North and South America. These are two separate continents and both are very diverse and large. The United States is in North America. We will spend more time learning about the United States in another year of study. Today we are just going to be introduced to these two contiennts.

 Read a continent books about North & South America

 Continent Study in Student Workbook

 Read out loud to your children. This is a great time to read historical books. Be sure to choose books that are written from a Christian perspective or audit them closely for anything that isn't God-glorifying and true. Children grades 1-5 should also spend time reading age-appropriate books.

CHECK LIST

- [ ] Worship
- [ ] Bible Reading
- [ ] Complete worksheets with each child
- [ ] Individual reading/reading out loud
- [ ] Math of choice

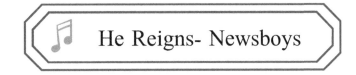

He Reigns- Newsboys

Read to student:

Today we will read about Ephesus. Ephesus is significant because it is the only place that we have a record in the Bible of letters written both by Paul and John to the Church there. This is a very neat chapter that we will read today. It speaks of the difference between the baptism of repentance and the baptism of Jesus and the Holy Spirit. It shows that believers in Jesus after Acts 2 were filled with the Holy Spirit, spoke in tongues, and prophesied (19:6). It speaks of the extraordinary miracles done by Paul and also cautions against trying to use the name of Jesus just for a miracle.

The riot at the end of the chapter shows what can happen when a group of people is stirred up. It is important that if we become passionate over an issue we really understand what it is about. We should never join a crowd yelling and carrying on about something we do not understand, and even if it is an issue we feel strongly about it is important to address it in the right way.

 Please pray with your kids. Encourage them to pray also.

Scripture Memory Acts 17:24-31

✓ While you read the Bible have your kids color their sheet in their workbook.

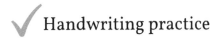 Bible Reading: Acts 19

Have the student(s) tell back what you read. Offer help along the way and kindly explain what you expect when they tell back a story. Be encouraging and compliment them.

✓ Handwriting practice

 # Science

On the sixth day of creation, God created animals that move on the ground and humans, who are created in the image of God. God made each kind of animal according to its kind and He said they were all good! What is your favorite animal? The study of animals is called zoology.

This week and next week we are going to focus on animals. We will choose one animal to study for next week, just as we did with fish and birds.

The last two weeks of our unit will be spent learning about humans, but I am guessing you already know a little bit about this since you are human! Always remember that we are created in God's image. We may share characteristics with animals, but humans are not animals. God gave humans dominion over the animals. He has good plans for each person. God knew you from before He formed you. The Bible is very clear on this truth!

CLASSIFICATION
SCIENCE ACTIVITY

We will need:
- A list of animals
- Paper
- Colored pencils
- Classification groups

Have your children draw pictures of their favorite animals. Make groups based on whether the animals are vertebrates or invertebrates.

- Discuss the differences in each group
- Discuss which are warm-blooded and which are cold-blooded
- Talk about other things that set these animals apart from each other
- Discuss where you would find each of these animals in creation

▶ Watch "Mammals for Kids" from Learn Bright on Youtube.

Note: This video uses wording about humans being animals. Please consider pointing out to your children that humans are not the same as animals although we are mammals.

No science worksheet this week.

Practical Learning Present these to your family without causing your kids to feel afraid. These are wise things we must teach.

- What do we do in the event of a fire? *Also teach stop, drop, and roll
- What do we do in the event of a natural disaster *fill in with applicable events such as earthquakes, tornadoes, or other.
- Should you ever go with a stranger? NO! Even if they tell you that they know your mom and dad you need to run and immediately come to find one of your parents.

 Language Arts Section in Student Workbook

 Observation Walk

Go on a walk outdoors and try to <u>observe</u> in creation what you <u>studied</u> in Science. Allow children to bring a notebook if they want to record their observations.
Use these three points to help start the discussion:

1

Look

Discuss what you are looking for.
Is there a location you could go to observe animals or perhaps their habitat?

2

Factor

Talk about the possibilities of seeing what you studied. Are there any animals you can spot outdoors? What classification do they fit into?

3

Observe

Did you find what you were looking for? Why? Why not? Did you learn something from seeing this in creation?

CHECK LIST

- ☐ Worship
- ☐ Bible Reading
- ☐ Individual reading/reading out loud
- ☐ Math of choice
- ☐ Complete worksheets with each child

 WEEK 1, DAY 4

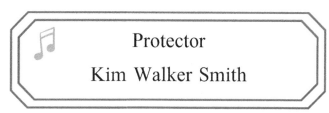
Protector

Kim Walker Smith

Read to student:

Let's play Bible trivia today! I am going to ask questions, you tell me the right answer as fast as you can. (In our family we offer chocolate chips or other small treats for correct answers. It makes Bible trivia extra sweet and the kids really enjoy it. If you are interested in more questions than are provided download our free Bible trivia printable on www.lampandlightmerchandise.com)

Bible Trivia

1. What day did God create the sun and moon?
2. Name one place Paul visited.
3. How long was Jesus in the grave before He rose?
4. Name one miracle Jesus performed.
5. How many tribes of Israel are there?
6. Say one of your memory verses.
7. What did God create on day 6?
8. How can we be saved?

 Please pray with your kids. Encourage them to pray also.

Scripture Memory Acts 17:24-31

 While you read the Bible have your kids color their sheet in their workbook.

📖 Bible Reading: Acts 20

Have the student(s) tell back what you read. Offer help along the way and kindly explain what you expect when they tell back a story. Be encouraging and compliment them.

✓ Handwriting Project   *Third and up write from memory.

At the end of each week have your student practice their best handwriting. Remove this sheet and share with a friend, family member, or persecuted/imprisoned Christian (send through Voice of the Martyrs). Have children 3rd and up address the envelope and write their return address.

Practical Learning

Have students repeat these facts after you. *Give practical examples and hands on demonstrations when possible and when needed.

- Say the Armor of God (Helmet of salvation, the breastplate of righteousness, the belt of truth, feet shod with the readiness of the gospel of peace, shield of faith, sword of the Spirit which is the Word of God.
- Measurement is broken down into units. An inch is a common unit of measurement. There are 12 inches in a foot, and 3 feet in a yard.

✓ Review anything from this week that your children struggled with. (Examples: Sight words, letters)

✓ Language Arts Section in Student Workbook

Read out loud to your children. This is a great time to read historical books. Be sure to choose books that are written from a Christian perspective or audit them closely for anything that isn't God-glorifying and true. Children grades 1-5 should also spend time reading age-appropriate books.

CHECK LIST

- ☐ Worship
- ☐ Bible Reading
- ☐ Complete worksheets with each child
- ☐ Individual reading/reading out loud
- ☐ Math of choice

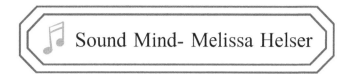
♪ Sound Mind- Melissa Helser

Read to student:

Paul knew that God had called him to preach in Rome although he knew hardships would come his way. He said yes to God even when it was going to be hard. Do you think you could say yes to God if He told you to do something difficult?

We can trust that God will be with us in anything that He calls us to do. There is nowhere that we go that He does not go with us. He is faithful!

 Watch "Bound for Rome: Acts 21-28" from The Bible Project on YouTube

Please pray with your kids. Encourage them to pray also.

Scripture Memory Acts 17:24-31

✓ While you read the Bible have your kids color their sheet in their workbook.

📖 Bible Reading: Acts 21

Have the student(s) tell back what you read. Offer help along the way and kindly explain what you expect when they tell back a story. Be encouraging and compliment them.

✓ Handwriting practice

✓ Language Arts Section in Student Workbook

Review + Focus

- What continent did we study in our last unit? Tell me one fact about it!
- How would you share the gospel with someone? Start with telling them who Jesus is. (Help as needed, encourage your kids to use what they practice to really share about Jesus with kids they encounter in your neighborhood, at the park, or otherwise.)
- Tell me one prayer that God has answered for you!
- Tell me one thing you are thankful for!

 Art Project:

*NOTE TO PARENTS: I don't know about you, but at our house, I receive many gifts of flowers over the summer months. Today our project is a sweet place for your children to put these.

Today we are going to make a flower board! You are going to design a vase on a piece of cardboard and when you gather flowers you will be able to poke them in these holes to create a pretty project.
To find ideas check Pinterest at @lampandlightliving, Unit 6 board.

Read out loud to your children. This is a great time to read historical books. Be sure to choose books that are written from a Christian perspective or audit them closely for anything that isn't God-glorifying and true. Children grades 1-5 should also spend time reading age-appropriate books.

CHECK LIST

- ☐ Worship
- ☐ Bible Reading
- ☐ Paint Story Rocks

- ☐ Individual reading/reading out loud
- ☐ Complete worksheets with each child
- ☐ Math of choice

 WEEK 2, DAY 2

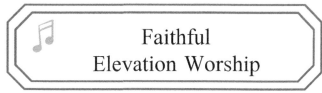
Read to student:

Yesterday we read about Paul in Jerusalem. Acts chapter 21 ends with Paul preparing to speak to the people. Today we will read what he said. Remember, there were Jewish people who did not believe that Jesus was the Messiah. Paul was Jewish, a Roman citizen, and also a Christian- a believer in Jesus.

Paul's heritage as a Jew gave him a certain amount of credibility with the Jewish people, but he also made them very mad at times.

Paul's rights as a Roman citizen afforded him certain treatment as well. Being an American citizen also affords us certain rights that are built into our government structure. Being a citizen of a certain place means you are either born there and have the rights afforded to people of that country or that you went through a process to permanently belong as one of their people. People who immigrate to America can become citizens but it takes time and is very expensive.

 Please pray with your kids. Encourage them to pray also.

Scripture Memory Acts 17:24-31

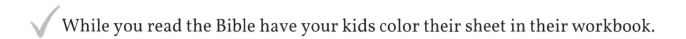

 While you read the Bible have your kids color their sheet in their workbook.

Bible Reading: Acts 22

Have the student(s) tell back what you read. Offer help along the way and kindly explain what you expect when they tell back a story. Be encouraging and compliment them.

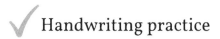 Handwriting practice

Practical Learning Have students repeat these facts after you.

- A penny is worth 1 cent, a nickel is worth 5 cents, a dime is worth 10 cents, a quarter is worth 25 cents.
- There are 100 cents in a dollar.
- For older kids challenge them to tell you what amount of money different combinations of coins makes.

✓ Language Arts Section in Student Workbook

 Read to student:

Do you remember what you learned last week about North and South America? Today we are going to have some fun with what we learned! We are going to make the information you learned into a visual report that you can share with others. There is a sheet in your workbook to help you get started.

Things to consider encouraging your child to add:
- Visual appeal with colors, themes, and facts
- Stickers, printed or magazine images, or drawings
- Number of countries
- Top natural resources
- Main religion, percent of known Christians *Be sure to share that this isn't always accurate if a country has laws against Christianity. We could have brothers and sisters in Christ not openly declaring their religion.
- Main bodies of water
- Any significant landmarks- both natural and man-made

Read out loud to your children. This is a great time to read historical books. Be sure to choose books that are written from a Christian perspective or audit them closely for anything that isn't God-glorifying and true. Children grades 1-5 should also spend time reading age-appropriate books.

CHECK LIST

- ☐ Worship
- ☐ Bible Reading
- ☐ Complete worksheets with each child
- ☐ Individual reading/reading out loud
- ☐ Math of choice

WEEK 2, DAY 3

N

Pour Your Spirit Out
Thrive Worship

Read to student:

As we read today I want you to notice Paul's respect for the High Priest of the Jewish people. Although Paul knew that Jesus was truly our High Priest for all time and all people by His blood that He shed on the cross, Paul still respected the position of the High Priest. We can honor someone's position even if we do not agree with what they do. We can show respect and pray for officials in high positions (1 Tim. 2:1-4) even if we view them as ungodly and bad for our country. Remember how we talked about being a citizen yesterday? The Bible says that as followers of Jesus, our most important citizenship is in heaven. We only live on this earth as sojourners and exiles, and ultimately we belong with Jesus! (Philippians 3:20, 1 Peter 2:9-12, Hebrew:11:13-15)

Notice how again the Lord appeared to Paul in the night to encourage him!

 Please pray with your kids. Encourage them to pray also.

Scripture Memory Acts 17:24-31

 While you read the Bible have your kids color their sheet in their workbook.

 Bible Reading: Acts 23

Have the student(s) tell back what you read. Offer help along the way and kindly explain what you expect when they tell back a story. Be encouraging and compliment them.

 Handwriting practice

 Science

Last week we learned about animals. This week you are going to choose one species to study. We are going to do research to understand the particulars of the animal you choose. We will learn about this animal, its habitat, what it eats, where it thrives, and much more!
Instead of doing an experiment, we will work on making a mini presentation about the animal you choose.

Practical Learning
Present these to your family without causing your kids to feel afraid. These are wise things we must teach.

- What do we do in the event of a fire? *Also teach stop, drop, and roll
- What do we do in the event of a natural disaster *Fill in with applicable events such as earthquakes, tornadoes, or other.
- Should you ever go with a stranger? NO! Even if they tell you that they know your mom and dad you need to run and immediately come to find one of your parents.

 Language Arts Section in Student Workbook

 ## Observation Walk

Go on a walk outdoors and try to <u>observe</u> in creation what you <u>studied</u> in Science. Allow children to bring a notebook if they want to record their observations.
Use these three points to help start the discussion:

1

Look

Discuss what you are looking for. Find the location around your outdoor environment with the highest probability.

2

Factor

Talk about the possibilities of seeing what you studied. Is there a place nearby where you can see this animal?

3

Observe

Did you find what you were looking for? Why? Why not? Did you learn something from seeing this in creation?

CHECK LIST

☐ Worship

☐ Bible Reading

☐ Complete worksheets with each child

☐ Individual reading/reading out loud

☐ Math of choice

 WEEK 2, DAY 4

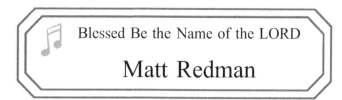
Blessed Be the Name of the LORD
Matt Redman

Read to student:

The Way, the beginning of what you and I know as Christianity, was originally a sect of Judaism. Christianity is not a new religion. It was the fulfillment of the long-awaited Messiah of the Hebrew/Jewish people. It is important for us to realize this as over the years it has separated so far from its roots that many think the Old Testament is entirely irrelevant. That could not be further from the truth! Do you remember what we learned about the Bereans last week? They were able to search the Old Testament and realize that Jesus is the Messiah. The most important change was the covenant made in Jesus' blood. This is the way for all people, whether Jew or Gentile to have access to God--through Jesus' sacrifice. Listen carefully to what Paul says today.

 Please pray with your kids. Encourage them to pray also.

Scripture Memory Acts 17:24-31

✓ While you read the Bible have your kids color their sheet in their workbook.

📖 Bible Reading: Acts 24

Have the student(s) tell back what you read. Offer help along the way and kindly explain what you expect when they tell back a story. Be encouraging and compliment them.

✓ Handwriting Project   *Third and up write from memory.

At the end of each week have your student practice their best handwriting. Remove this sheet and share with a friend, family member, or persecuted/imprisoned Christian (send through Voice of the Martyrs). Have children 3rd and up address the envelope and write their return address.

Practical Learning

Have students repeat these facts after you. *Give practical examples and hands on demonstrations when possible and when needed.

- Say the fruits of the Spirit: love, joy, peace, patience, kindness, goodness, faithfulness, gentleness, and self-control.
- Weight is how we know how heavy something is. An ounce is a small unit of weight. There are 16 ounces in a pound.

Read to student:

Give time for them to answer questions and remind them when needed.

Let's review what we have learned this week.

Can you tell me something we learned from the Bible?

Tell me one fact about North or South America?

Review anything from this week that your children struggled with. (Examples: sight words, letters)

Language Arts Section in Student Workbook

Read out loud to your children. This is a great time to read historical books. Be sure to choose books that are written from a Christian perspective or audit them closely for anything that isn't God-glorifying and true. Children grades 1-5 should also spend time reading age-appropriate books.

Help your child with their worksheet and report about a historical figure.

If you have not completed a book about a historical figure, do your best to help your child find a historical person of interest to use for this exercise. Add words your child may struggle with when writing to next week's spelling list.

CHECK LIST

- [ ] Worship
- [ ] Bible Reading
- [ ] Complete worksheets with each child
- [ ] Individual reading/reading out loud
- [ ] Math of choice

WEEK 3, DAY 1

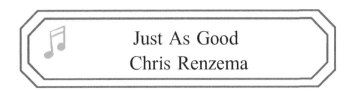
Read to student:

Paul spoke about Jesus before the important rulers of the day. He did so courageously, and I am certain he often remembered Jesus' reminder to "Take courage!"

There are governmental processes in place on this earth in most countries. There are often lower levels of government as well. In America, these levels are state government and local government which can vary from place to place. When Paul was going through the governmental systems he could confidently remember Daniel 2:20-21,

"Praise be to the name of God forever and ever;
    wisdom and power are his.
He changes times and seasons;
    he deposes kings and raises up others.
He gives wisdom to the wise
    and knowledge to the discerning."

Although we may have to deal with the government in our lifetime we can always remember that God is in control and our first allegiance always belongs to Him.

 Please pray with your kids. Encourage them to pray also.

Scripture Memory Acts 17:24-31

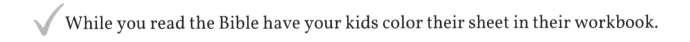 While you read the Bible have your kids color their sheet in their workbook.

📖 Bible Reading: Acts 25

Have the student(s) tell back what you read. Offer help along the way and kindly explain what you expect when they tell back a story. Be encouraging and compliment them.

Handwriting practice

 Language Arts Section in Student Workbook

Review
- How many days did it take God to create the world?
- Tell me the names of the continents.
- Do you remember your memory verse from last week?
- Tell me one thing you are thankful for!

Today for art we are going to make a sign that will help us remember that we obey God first and foremost. This can be a Bible verse, The Ten Commandments, or just a written reminder. We are going to work together to come up with a way we can do this. Here are some ideas to get started with, and you may also check @lampandlightliving on Pinterest and look at ideas on the Unit 6 board.

- Wood burn a sign
- Paint a sign
- Print and frame a sign
- Paint a canvas

Read out loud to your children. This is a great time to read historical books. Be sure to choose books that are written from a Christian perspective or audit them closely for anything that isn't God-glorifying and true. Children grades 1-5 should also spend time reading age-appropriate books.

 CHECK LIST

- [ ] Worship
- [ ] Bible Reading
- [ ] Paint Story Rocks

- [ ] Individual reading/reading out loud
- [ ] Complete worksheets with each child
- [ ] Math of choice

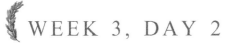
WEEK 3, DAY 2

Echo Holy
Red Rocks Worship

Read to student:

Do you know what a testimony is? A testimony is someone's story. When we say that someone is going to share their testimony as a Christian it is something that God did for them, usually to turn their hearts to Jesus for salvation. The book of Revelation says that we overcome by the blood of the Lamb (Jesus) and the word of our testimony. I like to think of what we are going to read today as Paul's testimony. He shared his story of encountering Jesus.

Paul showed confidence that must have come from God when his story was not kindly received. Instead of getting angry, rude, or silent, he calmly responded with the truth.

There is a verse that comes to mind when we read the end of Acts 26. King Agrippa asked Paul if he thought he could persuade him in such a short time to be a Christian. Our job as Christians is exactly that! Please look up and read 2 Corinthians 5:20. Our job as Christians is to make an appeal to the world to be reconciled to God.

 Please pray with your kids. Encourage them to pray also.

Scripture Memory Acts 17:24-31

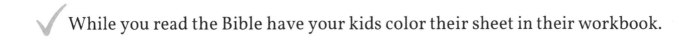 While you read the Bible have your kids color their sheet in their workbook.

 ## Bible Reading: Acts 26

Have the student(s) tell back what you read. Offer help along the way and kindly explain what you expect when they tell back a story. Be encouraging and compliment them.

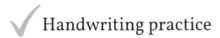 Handwriting practice

Practical Learning Have students repeat these facts after you.

- Freezing temperature of water is 32 degrees F.
- Boiling temperature of water is 212 degrees F.
- Water expands when it freezes.
- Water can be in different forms. It can be a liquid, a solid (ice), and a gas (steam).

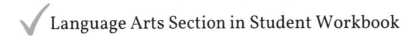 Language Arts Section in Student Workbook

 Read to student:

Today we are going to study one country from either North America or South America. If you have not already done so, please choose a country to study. We are going to work together to find the answers to the questions on your worksheet. Next week we will choose a project to do for the country you chose. You will have different options to choose from. You may look ahead in your book now and decide which project you will do. While we study, we will look for information to prepare for next week.

Every country is unique. They have distinct features both geographically and culturally. Some countries are very diverse. Take the United States for example. There are different areas of the United States that have very different cultures. How we talk even sounds a little bit different! Certain areas styles of food the vary, the climate varies, and the natural resources and job opportunities vary. While there is variation within a country, a country shares a common government, currency (money), main language, and laws.

Read out loud to your children. This is a great time to read historical books. Be sure to choose books that are written from a Christian perspective or audit them closely for anything that isn't God-glorifying and true. Children grades 1-5 should also spend time reading age-appropriate books.

CHECK LIST

- ☐ Worship
- ☐ Bible Reading
- ☐ Complete worksheets with each child
- ☐ Individual reading/reading out loud
- ☐ Math of choice

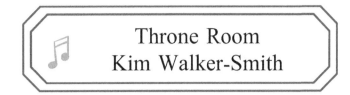
Throne Room
Kim Walker-Smith

Read to student:

Can you imagine what it would be like to be in a shipwreck? Paul had knowledge from God that he tried to share with those in charge of the ship he was sailing on. If those in charge had listened to Paul, the wreck would have been prevented, but they did not listen initially. Because they listened later, no one lost their life. Tomorrow we will find out what happened after the wreck, but for today we are going to read the story of Paul sailing for Rome

*If possible, use a map or a globe to show your children the route Paul traveled. This will help the route seem interesting instead of tedious. Show them the island of Malta, we will read more about it tomorrow.

 Please pray with your kids. Encourage them to pray also.

Scripture Memory Acts 17:24-31

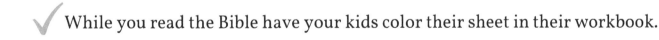 While you read the Bible have your kids color their sheet in their workbook.

📖 Bible Reading: Acts 27

Have the student(s) tell back what you read. Offer help along the way and kindly explain what you expect when they tell back a story. Be encouraging and compliment them.

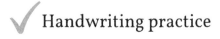 Handwriting practice

🔆 Science

What else did God create on day six of creation? That's right! People! Today we are going to study humans. Tell me one thing you already know about humans.

People are an incredibly fascinating thing to study. God created our bodies so intricately that it is hard to learn everything there is to know about the human body in just one day. We could spend an entire year learning about the human body! Today we will learn some of the basics. (Note: Science for Cycle 2 is a study of the human body.)

▶️ Watch "Human Body 101" from National Geographic on Youtube. *NOTE: The end of this video addresses the reproductive system, if you are not prepared to chat with your children about this you may wish to skip. Additionally, I do not support Nat Geo on a large scale.

✓ Science Activity and Worksheet

 # THE HUMAN BODY
SCIENCE ACTIVITY

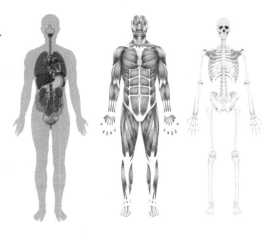

You will need:

- A measuring tape
- A scale
- Student workbook worksheet
- Ink pad

Your body has many systems that help it function well. For now, we are going to focus on some personal statistics about you! We are going to weigh you, measure you, trace your hand, take a fingerprint of one of your fingers, and you are going to draw a picture of yourself. There is no one on earth exactly like you. No one with your DNA and your fingerprints. You are uniquely created by God for good works which God prepared in advance for you to do!

*NOTE TO PARENTS: At the end of this I recommend praying for each of your children and speaking about their purpose as people created by God for a reason. Encourage them in their future and to seek God for what they should do. It is never too early to start this kind of training!

Practical Learning

- Each of the 50 states has a capital city. The capital of our state_____
- Washington D.C. is the capital of the United States.
- There are 12 tribes of Israel.
- Jesus had 12 disciples.

 Language Arts Section in Student Workbook

 ## Observation Walk

Go on a walk outdoors and try to <u>observe</u> in creation what you <u>studied</u> in Science. Allow children to bring a notebook if they want to record their observations.
Use these three points to help start the discussion:

| **1** | **2** | **3** |

Look

YOU are what we studied today.

Factor

Thank God for creating you the way you are and with the ability to move. Thank Him for creating people is His image.

Observe

Discuss how your body functions so that you are able to walk.

CHECK LIST

- [ ] Worship
- [ ] Bible Reading
- [ ] Complete worksheets with each child
- [ ] Individual reading/reading out loud
- [ ] Math of choice

He Reigns
Newsboys

Read to student:

Today we are finishing the book of Acts! It has been fun learning about the early church with you. I am so thankful they obeyed God and that we know about Jesus because of the faithfulness and obedience of those before us. We must make certain we continue to do our best to advance the kingdom of God and see the unreached reached with the Gospel. We will read about Paul's time on the island of Malta and what is believed to be the end of his life. He lived in Rome and shared the truth of Jesus there just as God called him to.

It is hard to even fathom the reach of Paul's ministry and how many believed in Jesus from among the Gentiles. We are abundantly blessed to know about Jesus and live where we can boldly and without hindrance proclaim Him. Let's do our best to look for opportunities to share Jesus! When we pray today let's ask God to provide these opportunities to us and provide courage and boldness for us.

Please pray with your kids. Encourage them to pray also.

Scripture Memory Acts 17:24-31

 While you read the Bible have your kids color their sheet in their workbook.

Bible Reading: Acts 28

Have the student(s) tell back what you read. Offer help along the way and kindly explain what you expect when they tell back a story. Be encouraging and compliment them.

 Handwriting Project   *Third and up write from memory.

At the end of each week have your student practice their best handwriting. Remove this sheet and share with a friend, family member, or persecuted/imprisoned Christian (send through Voice of the Martyrs). Have children 3rd and up address the envelope and write their return address.

Practical Learning

Have students repeat these facts after you. *Give practical examples and hands-on demonstrations when possible and when needed.

- Say the Lord's Prayer.
- Volume is another way we know how much of something there is, or how much is needed. We often use these in recipes. There are 8 ounces in one cup, 2 cups in a pint, 2 pints in a quart, and 4 quarts in a gallon.

Read to student:

Give time for them to answer questions and remind them when needed.

Let's review what we have learned this week.
Can you tell me something we learned from the Bible?
Tell me one fact about animals or humans that you have learned.

✓ Review anything from this week that your children struggled with. (Examples: sight words, letters)

✓ Language Arts Section in Student Workbook

📖 Read out loud to your children. This is a great time to read historical books. Be sure to choose books that are written from a Christian perspective or audit them closely for anything that isn't God-glorifying and true.

✓ Spend a few minutes with each child checking in on their reading progress. Make sure older children are able to decode words in syllables. Make sure younger children are recognizing their sight words within the text of a book.

CHECK LIST

- ☐ Worship
- ☐ Bible Reading
- ☐ Complete worksheets with each child
- ☐ Individual reading/reading out loud
- ☐ Math of choice

WEEK 4, DAY 1

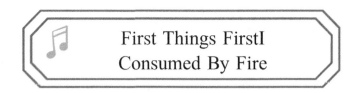
Read to student:

WOW! We are almost finished with our school year! This is our last week of structured learning. I have enjoyed teaching you. It is an honor to help you learn.

For our last week, we are going to study the book of Philippians. Paul wrote this letter to the Church at Philippi. If you remember, in Acts 16 we read about Paul visiting Philippi. It was a Roman colony and a leading city in that district of Macedonia (Acts 16:12). There, Paul spoke to women on the Sabbath who were praying by the river outside of the city gate. Paul and Silas were also in prison in Philippi and the Lord sent an earthquake to help with their release. We know that at very least the jailer and his family and Lydia and her family were the believers in Philippi after Paul passed through. By the time Paul wrote to the Church there, it seems the Church was well established. He mentions overseers and deacons which were a sign of an established Church. Paul also specifically mentioned two ladies in chapter four and another person. It is neat to realize the letters written to the Churches were to real people, many of whom Paul knew. Although they were written to real people they are also the timeless, alive, and active Word of God.

 Please pray with your kids. Encourage them to pray also.

Scripture Memory Acts 17:24-31

 While you read the Bible have your kids color their sheet in their workbook.

Bible Reading: Philippians 1

Have the student(s) tell back what you read. Offer help along the way and kindly explain what you expect when they tell back a story. Be encouraging and compliment them.

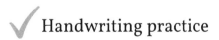 Handwriting practice

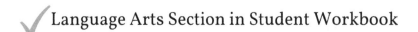 Language Arts Section in Student Workbook

Review

- Tell me one of the 10 Commandments.
- Tell me one fact about Africa.
- What makes a mammal a mammal?
- Tell me one thing you are thankful for!

 Today we are going to make a pretty arrangement of bird food/bird treats. Throughout the summer as we watch the birds enjoy what we have put out for them I want you to remember that we serve our God who cares for even the small birds and He cares much for you. Have faith in Him. He takes care of birds and flowers and you can trust Him to take care of you when you seek first His kingdom and His righteousness.

- Choose a style of bird food/feeder that you wish to make
- Look on the Unit 6 @lampandliving Pinterest board for ideas
- You may also wish to construct a bird house or purchase one that you allow your children to paint.

Read out loud to your children. This is a great time to read historical books. Be sure to choose books that are written from a Christian perspective or audit them closely for anything that isn't God-glorifying and true. Children grades 1-5 should also spend time reading age-appropriate books.

CHECK LIST

- [ ] Worship
- [ ] Bible Reading
- [ ] Art Project

- [ ] Individual reading/reading out loud
- [ ] Complete worksheets with each child
- [ ] Math of choice

 WEEK 4, DAY 2

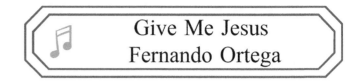
Read to student:

There are some challenging and important lessons in Philippians chapter 2! Having humility like Jesus is very important. God says many times in Scripture that pride is an abomination to Him and that He opposes the proud but give grace to the humble. We want to pray for humility and try to have tender hearts, because we know we are saved by grace and not of our own doing. We need to be cautious not to look down on others and not to think we are better than other people based on certain things that are of no value to God. In humility, we should count others as more important than ourselves (Philippians 2:3b).

We are to be different from the world by doing everything without complaining and arguing. Sometimes this is challenging. When we make mistakes we should repent to God and apologize to others. When we ask God to help us do better in an area He is faithful to help us and remind us of the right thing we desire to do through the Holy Spirit.

 Please pray with your kids. Encourage them to pray also.

Scripture Memory Acts 17:24-31

 While you read the Bible have your kids color their sheet in their workbook.

 Bible Reading: Philippians 2

Have the student(s) tell back what you read. Offer help along the way and kindly explain what you expect when they tell back a story. Be encouraging and compliment them.

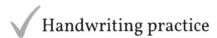 Handwriting practice

Practical Learning Have students repeat these facts after you.

- There are 5,280 feet in a mile.
- What did Jesus say the greatest commandments are? (Matt.
  1. Love the LORD your God with all your heart, soul, and strength
  2. The second is like it, love your neighbor as yourself.
     All of the Law and prophets hang on these two commands.

✓ Language Arts Section in Student Workbook

 Read to student:

Today we get to do our country project! Are you excited? Can you tell me why you chose the option you chose for our project? What is something that drew you to this country? Let's pray specifically for this country:

1. Pray for believers there to live for the Lord, love His Word, share the gospel, and seek first the kingdom of God.
2. Pray for their government officials to come to know Jesus and to have the wisdom to wisely lead their people. Pray for freedom to worship Jesus and peace.
3. Pray for missionaries in this country and leaders of God's people. Pray for safety and that they would not grow weary in doing good.
4. Pray for the Lord to send more gospel workers into the harvest. Jesus said the harvest is plentiful but the laborers few! (Matthew 9:35-38)

Note: Don't forget to have them present their project to a family member or friend.

✓ Geography Section in Student Workbook

Read out loud to your children. This is a great time to read historical books. Be sure to choose books that are written from a Christian perspective or audit them closely for anything that isn't God-glorifying and true. Children grades 1-5 should also spend time reading age-appropriate books.

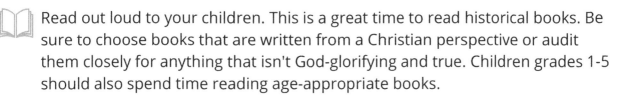

CHECK LIST

- ☐ Worship
- ☐ Bible Reading
- ☐ Complete worksheets with each child
- ☐ Individual reading/reading out loud
- ☐ Math of choice

WEEK 4, DAY 3

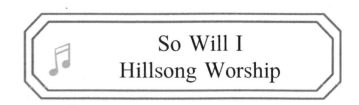
Read to student:

Do you remember how we read at the end of the book of Acts that Paul was in prison and then under house arrest? That is when he wrote this letter. Although Paul was in a tough situation, he still encouraged others and had his perspective shaped by the advancement of the kingdom of God. Consider that as we continue reading today.

▶ Watch "Overview: Philippians" from The Bible Project on Youtube.

 Please pray with your kids. Encourage them to pray also.

Scripture Memory Acts 17:24-31

✓ While you read the Bible have your kids color their sheet in their workbook.

📖 Bible Reading: Philippians 3

Have the student(s) tell back what you read. Offer help along the way and kindly explain what you expect when they tell back a story. Be encouraging and compliment them.

✓ Language Arts Section in Student Workbook

💡 Science

Last week we learned about the human body. This week you are going to choose one of the systems of the body to study. (Examples: skeletal, muscular, digestive, ext.) We will do research to understand the particulars of the system you choose. Instead of doing an experiment, we will work on making a mini presentation about the body system you choose.

Practical Learning

- Say the books of the Bible either from memory or with song.
- For students that are confident readers have them do a couple of Sword Drills. Sword Drills are fun competitions to see how fast you can find something in the Bible. Psalm 119:111, Zephaniah 3:17

 Language Arts Section in Student Workbook

 ## Observation Walk

Go on a walk outdoors and try to <u>observe</u> in creation what you <u>studied</u> in Science. Allow children to bring a notebook if they want to record their observations.
Use these three points to help start the discussion:

Look

Discuss how the body system you chose to study impacts your ability to walk.

Factor

How does this system work to help you walk? What if you suddenly lost this function?

Observe

Did you learn something experiencing this in creation?

CHECK LIST

- ☐ Worship
- ☐ Bible Reading
- ☐ Complete worksheets with each child
- ☐ Individual reading/reading out loud
- ☐ Math of choice

WEEK 4, DAY 4

Read to student:

You have learned so much this year. You have filled your heart and mind with truth from God's Word and this will be a blessing to you for the rest of your life. You have learned many things about our world and how to thrive as a sojourner in the world while living for God's kingdom to come. I am so happy we have gone on this learning adventure together. Thank you for the hard work that you have put into your studies. I am very thankful that the Lord entrusted you to our family.

You really never stop learning! I learned alongside you and you will continue learning over the summer. Use the tips and tactics we have practiced this year to ask good questions and to learn when you are outside enjoying creation.

Most importantly, I want you to remember that God loves you and He wants to lead you and guide you. You are never alone. He goes with you and the Holy Spirit dwells within you. No matter what you experience in your life you can do all things through Christ because He gives you strength.

 Please pray with your kids. Encourage them to pray also.

Scripture Memory Acts 17:24-31
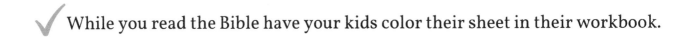

✓ **While you read the Bible have your kids color their sheet in their workbook.**

📖 **Bible Reading: Philippians 4**

Have the student(s) tell back what you read. Offer help along the way and kindly explain what you expect when they tell back a story. Be encouraging and compliment them.

✓ **Handwriting Project**   *Third and up write from memory.

At the end of each week have your student practice their best handwriting. Remove this sheet and share with a friend, family member, or persecuted/imprisoned Christian (send through Voice of the Martyrs). Have children 3rd and up address the envelope and write their return address.

End of unit review:

Give time for them to answer questions and remind them when needed.

Wow! Great job this week! I am enjoying teaching you and learning with you. Let's do a review of some of the things are have learned through this unit!

Can you tell me something we learned from the Bible?

Is there one verse or lesson that really helped you?
Did the LORD comfort or convict you in any area?

What is something you learned about animals or humans?

Tell me a historical person you most enjoyed learning about. Why did you enjoy their story?

What was your favorite thing you learned about North or South America?

✓ Review anything from this week that your children struggled with. (Examples: sight words, letters)

✓ Language Arts Section in Student Workbook

📖 Read out loud to your children. This is a great time to read historical books. Be sure to choose books that are written from a Christian perspective or audit them closely for anything that isn't God-glorifying and true.

✓ Spend a few minutes with each child checking in on their reading progress. Make sure older children are able to decode words into syllables. Make sure younger children are recognizing their sight words within the text of a book.

CHECK LIST

☐ Worship

☐ Bible Reading

☐ Complete worksheets with each child

☐ Individual reading/reading out loud

☐ Math of choice

WEEK 5

Mini-Unit Study Plan

✓ Choose a topic

✓ Find needed resources- videos, websites, books

✓ Choose activities: field trip, experiment, movie

✓ Find Scriptures that may apply

Plan

Work with your child(ren) to come up with the best study for your family. Make a plan and allow them to be involved in finding resources and ideas.

Learn

Choose ways that learning will be involved. Examples include a write up, making lists, books to read, and more

Enjoy

Have fun! Allow your child to talk to others about their experience. Try to enjoy this week together and foster a desire to learn more.

WEEK 5 DAILY CHECK LIST

☐ Unit Study   ☐ Math of choice

☐ Unit Study   ☐ Math of choice

☐ Unit Study   ☐ Math of choice

☐ Unit Study   ☐ Math of choice

Congratulations!

Good job on a school year founded on God's Word!
Thank you so much for trusting me with the job of producing a curriculum for your children. This is a huge undertaking and indeed was not possible on my own. I pray this has been a fruitful school year for you and your children. May it produce a kingdom harvest of righteousness for years to come.

Extras

EDITING/GRADING
Checklist

This list is designed to help you, as a parent, check your child's writing for substance and grammar. Be constructive in your criticism. Compliment often. I find this area to be challenging as a homeschool mom. I want to encourage my children as their mom but also to push them to do their best and to improve as their teacher. Different personalities respond differently to this dynamic. Don't be afraid to kindly remind your child that during school you are their teacher. They will need to have the humility to allow you to correct them, while still valuing their achievements. Please use this list as you correct your child's writing assignments.

☐ Sentence structure
  - Does every sentence flow well?
  - Does every sentence make sense?
  - Does every sentence sound right?
  - Does every sentence have a noun and a verb in their proper tense?

☐ Spelling (Don't forget to add misspelled words to your child's weekly spelling list)

☐ Proper use of words- check for proper use of homophones, especially common ones such as there/their, to/too/two, are/our

☐ Capital letters- beginning letter of each sentence, proper nouns, the word I

☐ Creative word use- make suggestions for improving word selection to be more engaging and interesting

☐ Check for run-on sentences

☐ Check for fragment sentences

☐ Proper punctuation including periods, question marks, commas, semicolons, and quotations.

☐ Indentation of paragraphs

☐ Paragraph structure and content

☐ Is the main idea conveyed well?

PRONOUNS

I	he	some
me	him	many
my	his	each
they	she	other
their	her	others
theirs	hers	what
them	this	who
we	that	whom
us	these	whose
our	those	
ours	all	
it	any	
its	both	

A pronoun is a word that is used instead of a noun.

PARTS OF SPEECH

NOUN - is a word that names a person, place, thing, or event.

VERB - is a word that denotes an action or state of being.

ADJECTIVE - is a word that describes or modifies a noun.

ADVERB - is a word that modifies a verb, an adjective, or another adverb.

PRONOUN - is a word that is used to replace a noun in a sentence.

PREPOSITION - is a word that shows the relationship between a noun or a pronoun in a sentence.

CONJUNCTION - is a word that connects words, phrases, or sentences.

INTERJECTION - is a word that shows an intense feeling or emotion.

PUNCTUATION

PERIOD
Marks the end of a sentence.

COMMA
A pause or short break in a sentence.

Indicates that the sentence is a question.

COLON
Introduces information that adds meaning to the text before the colon.

SEMICOLON
Joins two independent clauses.

QUOTATION
Spoken words within text that signify dialogue.

EXCLAMATION
Marks the end of an exclamatory sentence to express strong emotions.

APOSTROPHE
The omission of letters to shorten a word. Also used for pluralising words.

PARENTHESES
A pair of enclosed punctuation marks that provide additional information about the sentence.

ELLIPSIS
Indicates missing information, a pause in speech, or a trail off...

Meghann's Thank You Notes ♡

I would like to thank God first and foremost for choosing someone as unequipped as myself to take on this task. Reading Scripture gave me just enough confidence to know that when the "wrong" person for a job is called, God equips them. To the praise and glory of God alone, I can say that is the case with this project. He has continued to faithfully provide every step of the way. Without the indwelling of the Holy Spirit, there is no way you would have this curriculum. God has consistently taught me a deeper trust in Him through making this.

Thank you to my precious family. My husband graciously trusts me to educate our children and allowed me to create this curriculum to school them. Like many parents, his children are his greatest joy. I do not take lightly that he trusts me with this task. His willingness to allow me to pour time and resources into this project is an incredible blessing. To each of our children- thank you! You continue to bring so much inspiration to this project, and I hope that our time using it to school you will play a role in helping you to love the Lord and His Word! A special thanks to our oldest son, Angler. Buddy, I sure appreciate your help with activities, sight words, and all of the different ways you helped me both on paper and in the house while I was writing!

God's provision for our needs continues to astound me. Editing is not my forte. Sara Sweigard, thank you <u>SO</u> much for reaching out and being willing to step out in obedience to fill a huge need For That It May Go Well. I sincerely appreciate your time editing. This testimony is the cherry on top of God's faithfulness in this work! We serve a mighty and faithful Father. When He asks you to step out in faith He provides every step of the way and many times the way He does that is through our brothers and sisters in Christ. Sara, it is an honor and immense blessing to have you editing these books!

God is faithful, may He get all the glory. TRUST HIM!

Made in the USA
Coppell, TX
11 October 2024